CHARLYT

MW00617707

A
Daily
Devotional

Hope For Hurting Marriages

By

Charlyne A. Steinkamp

CHARLYNE CARES

A Daily Devotional

Published by Rejoice Ministries, Inc.
P. O. Box 11242
Pompano Beach, Florida 33061

Scripture quotations are from the King James Version
Or the Holy Bible, New International Version,
Copyright 1984, International Bible Society
Used by permission.

Verses marked TLB are taken from The Living Bible,
Copyright, 1971. Used by permission of
Tyndale House Publishers, Inc., Wheaton, Illinois 60189
All rights reserved.

Printed in the United States of America

BUTTERFLIES

A STORY ABOUT THE COVER

Butterflies will have two metamorphoses, (or transformations) in their lifetime. A butterfly's life begins as an egg from which is hatched the caterpillar (or larva). A newly hatched caterpillar eats a lot. As it grows, it gets too big for its skin or exoskeleton and sheds it. This process is called molting and can happen as many as eight times--as few as four. When the caterpillar is fully grown, it hangs its body from a twig. It then sheds its skin the last time. The skin splits and reveals a greenish-yellow, soft pupa or chrysalis. The pupa's soft surface hardens quickly into a protective shell. Inside, the caterpillar is becoming a butterfly. But even scientists don't know how this transformation takes place. This process can take a few days or months--some require up to a year. New butterfly growers were urged not to give up on a chrysalis which seemed to be dead--give it more time.

When the metamorphosis is complete, the butterfly pushes hard against its protective shell. The head emerges almost immediately, and eventually the whole butterfly works itself free and grips the outside of the shell. The soft wings expands, hanging down. A fluid is pumped into their veins, and the wings begin to set. If the wings are touched at this stage, they will be deformed forever.

Butterflies drink a syrupy liquid called nectar which they extract from flowers. Butterflies need the sun to warm their wings--then they gather nectar from flower to flower pollinating flowers as they go and giving life.

We, as standers, can learn from the butterfly. We need to wait patiently as our mate is transformed into a new creature (2 Corinthians 5:17) in his or her chrysalis. They are not dead, but are being transformed. Our eyes would love to peer in and see, but it's a secret project directed by the Creator.

Even as their head emerges and they start to "think" about home, their body could still be stuck in the circumstances. They <u>will emerge!</u> New life fluids (God's spirit of healing) (Ezekiel 11:19) will pump through their limp, fragile wings. It is important for us, as standers, not to impede the Holy Spirit's work. Our mates will be very fragile at that time. We must give the Holy Spirit time to heal them and set their "wings."

How glorious it will be to see our newly transformed mates warming their wings in the presence of the "Son" of God and then someday bringing life to others.

By Karen Lewis, a stander from Anaheim, California

IN APPRECIATION

God is so good. Each time He births an idea for a new book, He provides volunteers to help us accomplish the task. We are fortunate to have several friends who have helped make this book become a reality.

This is the third manuscript Julie Bell has typed for us. Looking at the completed book, it is easy to forget the hours of typing, retyping, and making changes that are required before publishing. Even after all the phone calls and overnight mailings, there is always just one final change. Thank you, Julie, for your work, always done as unto the Lord. The extras that you add to the pages do so much!

Several years ago, the Lord allowed us to meet Karen Lewis, a stander, in California. Karen has provided us with beautiful and touching art work for several book covers. She is always ready to put on paper the concept Bob or I have in mind. This book also contains Karen's comments regarding this cover.

Our friend, Norman Kane, of Melody Printing Company, in Pompano Beach, Florida, has a heart and a burden for the work of Rejoice Ministries. The cover of this book is the sixth one he has designed for us. Norman, thank you for everything you do for us!

We could not print books without faithful friends who volunteer hours to read and reread the manuscript. These special people are: Vicki Aurswald, Sandra Hinsley, Kimberly Kuebler, Lorrie Meininger, Paula Roberts, Faye Sickler, and Donna Smith.

Our greatest appreciation goes to friends who prayed this book into becoming a reality, and those who contributed toward printing expenses.

May God richly bless each of you.

DEDICATION

This book is dedicated to a very special woman of faith and prayer warrior, Marilyn Conrad, who prays fervently for so many prodigals who have left their spouses and their families to go to the "far country."

When "marriage ministry" is mentioned, often the first name that comes to mind is Marilyn Conrad, founder of Covenant Keepers, Inc., in Tulsa, Oklahoma. After her own home was attacked several years ago, she searched the Scriptures to gain God's perspective on marriage and divorce. As a result, she opened her home to others in the same situation. She also began to volunteer for a marriage healing ministry and later went on staff for four years.

Covenant Keepers is the result of those years of ministry to others and the Biblical principles she learned during that time. Today, the ministry she founded helps thousands around the world.

Since the birth, of Rejoice Ministries, eight years ago, Marilyn has not only been a co-laborer, but a supporter, as well. She has come to Florida to attend and speak at our retreats. Marilyn has also opened the podium at her conferences for us to speak. This book will first be introduced at the Rejoice Ministries book table at Covenant Keepers.

Marilyn, Charlyne cares because you taught me, by example, how to care for hurting people as well as showing so many your faith and your perseverance for the restoration of marriages around the world.

It is with love and appreciation for all that you have done and are doing for the restoration and reconciliation of marriages that this book is dedicated to you.

May the Lord richly bless you and your marriage.

A Sister in the Lord,

Charlyne

Praise be to the God and Father of our Lord Jesus Christ, the Father of compassion and the God of all comfort, who comforts us in all our troubles, so that we can comfort those in any trouble with the comfort we ourselves have received from God. 2 Corinthians 1:3-4

INTRODUCTION

What a privilege it is to prepare daily devotions and send them out on the Internet. My husband, Bob, and I have many friends who are believing for a miracle in their marriage, but who do not have Internet access. This book is especially for them. The Lord wants to restore and rebuild your marriage on the solid rock of Jesus Christ. The title of this book comes from the hearts of the Steinkamps; Charlyne cares and Bob cares.

I pray these few pages will give you hope and encouragement in your daily devotional time. They have been arranged so that you will have one for each day of the week.

I pray that as you read the Scriptures, they will increase your faith giving you a new hope and encouragement regardless of your circumstances. Cry out to your Lord and meet Him in a new way you have never known Him. Deepen your relationship with Him. He will never leave NOR forsake you. As you spend time with the Lord, praise and worship Him, for He is truly a mighty, awesome God.

You may read many books about marriage, but the greatest book you can ever read is the Bible. I found that as I read the Scriptures, the Lord directed me in my daily life. He taught me His principles and precepts. He increased my faith and trust--molding me and making me into a new woman in the Lord. I challenge each of you to read, to study, and to meditate on the Word and you will get excited with how the Lord shows you something new each day!

Seek and grow in the Lord as you wait patiently for God's perfect timing to bring your prodigal home. The Lord loves your spouse so very much. He is calling your spouse every day telling the one you love to come home, home to God and to a waiting and praying family.

Believe in the power of your God. Believe in a miracle!

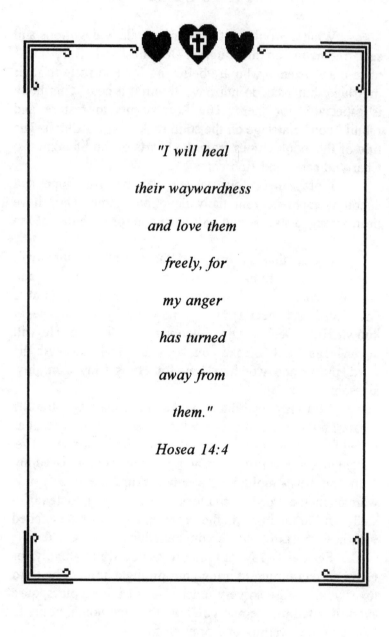

"I will heal

their waywardness

and love them

freely, for

my anger

has turned

away from

them."

Hosea 14:4

♥ MONDAY ♥

From that time on Jesus began to preach, "Repent, for the kingdom of heaven is near." Matthew 4:17

On Sunday, our pastor talked about repenting. Repent means: To have a change of mind; a feeling of regret or remorse; turning away from sin and back to God. As I was listening, I started thinking about all the prodigals that need to repent and turn from their wicked ways. Oh, my prayer is that all of our churches, all of our Christian radio stations, and all of our Christian television programs would continue to cry out, "Repent!" May we all pray in agreement that ALL prodigals will REPENT!

Once we repent, our Lord Jesus Christ will change each person from the inside out. They will be set free from the bondages of sin.

Pray that all our spouses and loved ones this week will REPENT and be OBEDIENT to the Lord's voice.

Read Jeremiah 7:1-11 and Romans 6.

I praise the Lord that He can set ALL prodigals free through the blood of our Lord Jesus Christ.

But now that you have been set free from sin and have become slaves to God, the benefit you reap leads to holiness, and the result is eternal life. For the wages of sin is death, but the gift of God is eternal life in Christ Jesus our Lord. Romans 6:22-23.

Peter replied, "Repent and be baptized, every one of you, in the name of Jesus Christ for the forgiveness of your sins. And you will receive the gift of the Holy Spirit. The promise is for you and your children and for all who are far off--for all whom the Lord our God will call." With many other words he warned them; and he pleaded with them, "Save yourselves from this corrupt generation."
Acts 2:38-40

May we not become weary in all that we do for the Lord. May each of us continue to cry, *"Thy will be done."* May we pray repentance for all prodigals and loved ones. May we never forget the power of our Lord Jesus Christ.

Do not be deceived: God cannot be mocked. A man reaps what he sows. The one who sows to please his sinful nature, from that nature will reap destruction; the one who sows to please the Spirit, from the Spirit will reap eternal life. Let us not become weary in doing good, for at the proper time we will reap a harvest if we do not give up. Therefore, as we have opportunity, let us do good to all people, especially to those who belong to the family of believers.Galatians 6:7-10

But those who hope in the Lord, will renew their strength. They will soar on wings like eagles; they will run and not grow weary, they will walk and not be faint. Isaiah 40:31

♥ WEDNESDAY ♥

Today, remember that your Lord loves you and your spouse. He will continue to call your spouse back to Him. He desires to have a personal relationship with you and your spouse.

Read Ezekiel 34.

" 'For this is what the Sovereign Lord says: I myself will search for my sheep and look after them. As a shepherd looks after his scattered flock when he is with them, so will I look after my sheep. I will rescue them from all the places where they were scattered on a day of clouds and darkness. I will bring them out from the nations and gather them from the countries, and I will bring them into their own land. I will search for the lost and bring back the strays. I will bind up the injured and strengthen the weak....' "
Ezekiel 34:11-13, 16

Remember that Jesus said, *"I have not come to call the righteous, but sinners to repentance."* Luke 5:32

God loves you and knows right where your spouse is today. Trust Him to bring your spouse home!

Pray for your spouse to repent and turn from their wicked ways. The world is not calling sin--sin. May the Lord send messengers to speak the truth--and the truth WILL set your spouse free!

♥ THURSDAY ♥

God is our refuge and strength, an ever-present help in trouble. Psalm 46:1

Your Lord is so faithful. Daily we hear of praise reports from people who have previously written a letter of desperation. Your Lord hears your cries and your needs. God is always there waiting to help you regardless of your present circumstances. He wants to provide you with refuge, security, and peace beyond your understanding. You need to know that your Lord God has power to handle every one of your present day problems. You need to have complete confidence in whom you serve. Do you really believe in the power of your Lord?

Read Psalm 46.

"Be still, and know that I am God; I will be exalted among the nations, I will be exalted in the earth." The Lord Almighty is with us; the God of Jacob is our fortress. Psalm 46:10-11

Take time today to be still and praise your Lord for all that He is doing for you and for your family. Talk to Him as if He were your best friend. Tell Him all your concerns, your fears, and your anxieties. Ask Him for His daily direction for all of your needs. Remember, **He has a plan and a purpose for you and for your family. Trust Him. He will never fail you!**

"For I know the plans I have for you," declares the Lord, "plans to prosper you and not to harm you, plans to give you hope and a future." Jeremiah 29:11

♥ FRIDAY ♥

Show me your ways, O Lord, teach me your paths; guide me in your truth and teach me, for you are God my Savior, and my hope is in you all day long. Remember not the sins of my youth and my rebellious ways; according to your love remember me, for you are good, O Lord. Guard my life and rescue me; let me not be put to shame, for I take refuge in you. May integrity and uprightness protect me, because my hope is in you." Psalm 25:4-5, 7, 20-21

So many times during our walk with the Lord, we fall spiritually. May we always remember that our Lord will direct our every step, if we will just ask Him. He is always with us and will never forsake us.

If the Lord delights in a man's way, he makes his steps firm; though he stumble, he will not fall, for the Lord upholds him with his hand. Psalm 37:23-24

In his heart a man plans his course, but the Lord determines his steps. Proverbs 16:9

May we always remember that even though our spouse says, "I am never coming home," **our Lord directs their steps. He has the power to orchestrate anything He desires.** May we always continue to believe that our Lord is determining these steps of both you and your prodigal every day. Do not be afraid of what the future holds. His plan is the best one!

I know, O Lord, that a man's life is not his own; it is not for man to direct his steps. Jeremiah 10:23

May your prayer today be that we will be sensitive to His direction in your lives. Listen to the Holy Spirit's soft voice throughout the day. Pray that your Lord will continue to direct your family's steps each day.

♥ 5 ♥

Are you discouraged this weekend? Many of our standers let the enemy come in on the weekend to cause depression, despair, tiredness, and fear. Where are you today?

Bob and I know that your circumstances may seem overwhelming today.

Read Joshua 1.

The Lord says, *"I will never leave you nor forsake you."* Joshua 1:5

Prayer is the key to handling discouragement. Throughout the Bible, there are people who were discouraged, feeling their circumstance was impossible and hopeless. Is that how you feel?

Read I Samuel 1:1-28, Nehemiah 4:1-14, and Philippians 1:12-30.

Prayer opens the way for God to work. Tell God how you really feel and leave your problems with Him. Remind yourself who you serve--a Mighty God.

Your Lord has a plan and a purpose for you and your spouse. Stand in the gap for them.

In each circumstance, we choose to praise the Lord or to complain. How are you reacting to your circumstances? Ask the Holy Spirit to change your attitude to be more like Jesus.

Do not be discouraged this weekend--look for a rainbow.

"Have I not commanded you? Be strong and courageous. Do not be terrified; do not be discouraged, for the Lord your God will be with you wherever you go." Joshua 1:9

♥ SUNDAY ♥

I rejoiced with those who said to me, "Let us go to the house of the Lord." Psalm 122:1

May today be a special day with the Lord.
Our prayer is that you will receive a special blessing when you worship the Lord.

Read Psalm 146.

Give thanks to the Lord, for He is good; His love endures forever. Psalm 107:1

Blessed are they whose ways are blameless, who walk according to the law of the Lord. Blessed are they who keep his statutes and seek him with all their heart. I seek you with all my heart; do not let me stray from your commands. I have hidden your word in my heart that I might not sin against you. Psalm 119:1-2, 10-11

Praise be to the Lord, the God of Israel, from everlasting to everlasting. Let all the people say, "Amen!" Praise the Lord. Psalm 106:48

HAVE A BLESSED DAY WITH THE LORD.

Do you really believe in the power of prayer?

I remember 12 years ago, when my marriage was totally demolished and over by the world's standards, **I cried out to my Lord. He heard my cries and started answering my prayers in ways that I never dreamed possible.**

Bob gave me two books for my birthday that I have already started reading. One book is: Too Busy Not To Pray by Bill Hybels and the other book is: Putting Your Past Behind You by Erwin W. Lutzer. While I am reading, I am thinking, "Oh, this is so good I need to share this with our people."

If we all really knew the power of prayer, many of us would spend much more time praying.

"Truly, truly, I say to you, if you ask the Father for anything in my name, he will give it to you. Until now you have asked for nothing in my name; ask and you will receive, so that your joy may be made full." John 16:23-24

Erwin W. Lutzer states, "We have the authority we need to be free of demonic control. To be able to destroy strongholds--to demolish the power of the enemy. We've learned that effective warfare means we have the resources not just to resist the enemy, but also to rout him from his entrenched positions. This can be done only in the name of someone stronger than satan, stronger than our past, our sins, and our memories. To pray in Christ's name is to apply His victory boldly in a specific situation."

Let's commit ourselves to the power of prayer and keep praying, taking back from satan the territory he has taken!

Have a great week praying for your family!

♥ TUESDAY ♥

The effective prayer of a righteous man can accomplish much. James 5:16

If you could ask God for one miracle in your life, knowing that He would grant your request, what would it be? Whatever your request might be, do you regularly and diligently, every single day, bring it to God in prayer, trusting that He will intervene in your situation? Are you weary and tired of praying? Bob and I are here to encourage you about the power of prayer. We want to be like Aaron and Hur, who upheld Moses' arms when he became weary.

Read Exodus 17: 8-16.

When Moses' hands grew tired, they took a stone and put it under him and he sat on it. Aaron and Hur held his hands up--one on one side, one on the other--so that his hands remained steady till sunset. So Joshua overcame the Amalekite army with the sword. Exodus 17:12-13

You can overcome the evil one by the sword of the Spirit, which is the Word of God.

Take the helmet of salvation and the sword of the Spirit, which is the word of God. Ephesians 6:17

You can be strong in the Lord. Believe in the power of prayer. Know that others are beside you holding up your arms in praise, in thanksgiving, in honor, and in glory of the Sovereign Lord you serve. He will never fail you or your family!

Do you have peace even in the midst of your present circumstances? My prayer is that you will ask and receive peace from your Lord today.

My prayer for you is in **Numbers 6:24-26.**

"The Lord bless you and keep you; the Lord make his face shine upon you and be gracious to you; the Lord turn his face toward you and give you peace."

The world cannot provide you peace. **Real peace comes from faith in God. To find peace of mind and peace with others, you must find peace with God.**

"Peace I leave with you; my peace I give you. I do not give to you as the world gives. Do not let your hearts be troubled and do not be afraid." John 14:27

Do not be anxious about anything, but in everything, by prayer and petition, with thanksgiving, present your requests to God. And the peace of God, which transcends all understanding, will guard your hearts and your minds in Christ Jesus. Philippians 4:6-7

Many of you may become anxious about different circumstances, finances, and family situations, but may these scriptures encourage you today that the Lord wants you to lay your problems at His feet and trust Him completely to solve all of them.

Now may the Lord of peace himself give you peace at all times and in every way. 2 Thessalonians 3:16

Are you tired of waiting? Many of you are having to wait for GOD'S TIMING for your marriage to be restored. Let me reassure you, that it is worth waiting for. **Your marriage being restored is WORTH IT!!**

"But if it were I, I would appeal to God; I would lay my cause before him. He performs wonders that cannot be fathomed, miracles that cannot be counted." Job 5:8-9

Great is the Lord and most worthy of praise; His greatness no one can fathom. One generation will commend your works to another; they will tell of your mighty acts. They will speak of the glorious splendor of your majesty, and I will meditate on your wonderful works. They will tell of the power of your awesome works, and I will proclaim your great deeds. Psalm 145:3-6

Wait for the Lord; be strong and take heart and wait for the Lord. Psalm 27:14

Did you know that David was anointed as a king at the age of sixteen, but didn't become the king until he was thirty? **David had to wait on God for the fulfillment of His promise to reign. So let us wait and believe in the power of our Lord Jesus Christ to restore your marriage. Most of all, pray for your spouse's salvation.**

The Lord is good to those whose hope is in him, to the one who seeks him; it is good to wait quietly for the salvation of the Lord. Lamentations 3:25-26

You need to persevere so that when you have done the will of God, you will receive what he has promised. Hebrews 10:36

When they reached the place God had told him about, Abraham built an altar there and arranged the wood on it. He bound his son Isaac and laid him on the altar, on top of the wood. Then he reached out his hand and took the knife to slay his son. But the angel of the Lord called out to him from heaven, "Abraham! Abraham!" "Here I am," he replied. "Do not lay a hand on the boy," he said. "Do not do anything to him. Now I know that you fear God, because you have not withheld from me your son, your only son." Genesis 22:9-12

Today, be like Abraham, trusting and obeying your Lord. **Are you willing to obey the Lord regardless of the sacrifice?** Ask the Lord what He wants you to do. **I believe standing for your loved ones is a sacrifice with heavenly rewards!**

Read Genesis 22:1-9. What a powerful story about a man of faith!

Was not our ancestor Abraham considered righteous for what he did when he offered his son Isaac on the altar? You see that his faith and his actions were working together, and his faith was made complete by what he did. And the scripture was fulfilled that says, "Abraham believed God, and it was credited to him as righteousness," and he was called God's friend. James 2:21-23

Abraham said in *Genesis 22:5, "We will worship and then we will come back to you."* He expected God to do a miracle. Are you expecting a miracle? Live everyday expecting your spouse to come home.

Have a great day asking the Lord what He wants you to do!

So Abraham called that place The Lord Will Provide. And to this day it is said, "On the mountain of the Lord it will be provided." Genesis 22:14

I know that many of you get discouraged because you do not see any evidence of change in your spouse. We all could get discouraged very easily by looking at all the every day circumstances. I often cry out to the Lord and ask Him how I should pray for all the prodigals in the world. I have felt led to regularly pray Psalm 51 by praying it as a prayer for all the prodigals and standers and all their loved ones in the world.

Would you like to join me in agreement? This is a psalm where David had not only committed adultery but also murder. Then David repented and the Lord touched him and used him mightily in the future. May all the prodigals be used by the Lord in the very near future.

Today ask the Lord what He wants you to accomplish for yourself and for someone else this weekend!

Have mercy on me, O God, according to your unfailing love; according to your great compassion blot out my transgressions. Psalm 51:1

Cleanse me with hissop, and I will be clean; wash me, and I will be whiter than snow. Let me hear joy and gladness; let the bones you have crushed rejoice. Psalm 51:7-8

Restore to me the joy of your salvation and grant me a willing spirit, to sustain me. Then I will teach transgressors your ways, and sinners will turn back to you. Psalm 51:12-13

O Lord, open my lips, and my mouth will declare your praise. Psalm 51:15

♥ SUNDAY ♥

Be transformed by the renewing of your mind. Romans 12:2

Today, as we worship our Lord, may we say a prayer. "Lord, change me, renew me, and remold me. Lord, give me the mind of Christ. May I surrender my will to do Your will and Your way in my life each and every day."

Therefore, I urge you, brothers, in view of God's mercy to offer your bodies as living sacrifices, holy and pleasing to God--this is your spiritual act of worship. Do not conform any longer to the pattern of this world, but be transformed by the renewing of your mind. Then you will be able to test and approve what God's will is--his good, pleasing and perfect will. Romans 12:1-2

As you know, we are burdened for you, and your spouse who is away from God's will. Yesterday, I heard the above scripture given at a women's seminar. I was blessed in a couple of ways. First, I have heard of Nancy Missler and have a couple of her books: Be Ye Transformed and Why Should I Be The First To Change?, but never had heard her in person. Second, she has a restored, healed marriage! PTL!

She shared her testimony and principles the Lord has taught her in the Bible.

I was blessed. I came home and shared with Bob and thought how Nancy and I are both blessed by having restored marriages. You can have a restored marriage if you will make a decision to follow your Lord's will. You have a choice each day to be more like Jesus. Frequently, ask yourself with all your present circumstances, "What Would Jesus Do?" Ask the Lord to show you His will and His way for your life.

Be sure to spend time with the Lord this Sunday.

How would you grade your prayer time? Do your prayers sound like, "Lord, I need this, give me that, help me with this, and solve this?" We may toss in a few thanks, throw in a little worship, and even confess a couple of sins. Do you have a regular time you spend praying daily with your Lord? Do you have a prayer journal or a prayer list? Your prayer life may be out of balance. Let me suggest a prayer pattern using A.C.T.S. This practice is common to many but new to others.

A: Adoration
C: Confession
T: Thankfulness
S: Supplication or requests

Begin by *adoring* your Lord. Think of His wonderful character. Tell Him how much you love Him. You serve an awesome, mighty God.

Read Psalm 145.

Continue with a *confession* of anything in your life that might not please the Lord. Confess your need of Him. Talk to your Heavenly Father as if He is right beside you (because He is). Confess all your thoughts, concerns, worries, and needs. Visualize them, putting them at His feet. Then leave them there, so He can solve and provide for your every need.

Cast all your anxiety on him because he cares for you.
I Peter 5:7

Let us then approach the throne of grace with confidence, so that we may receive mercy and find grace to help us in our time of need. Hebrews 4:16

May you always remember the power of prayer as you look at the final part of A.C.T.S.

After adoring the Lord and confessing your need of Him, **thank** Him for what He has done, is doing, and is going to do in your life and the lives of those you love.

I will praise God's name in song and glorify him with thanksgiving. This will please the Lord. Psalm 69:30, 31a

Find your time in prayer by bringing your **supplications** or requests before the Lord.

Do not be anxious about anything, but in everything by prayer and petition, with thanksgiving, present your requests to God. Philippians 4:6

Your Father knows what you need before you ask him. Matthew 6:8

This is the confidence we have in approaching God: that if we ask anything according to his will, he hears us. I John 5:14

Remember how often your Lord prayed and the pattern He gave us to follow.

Read Matthew 6:6-15

"This, then, is how you should pray:
" 'Our Father in heaven,
hallowed be your name,
your kingdom come, your will be done
on earth as it is in heaven.
Give us today our daily bread.
Forgive us our debts,
as we forgive our debtors.
And lead us not into temptation,
but deliver us from the evil one.' " Matthew 6:9-13

♥ WEDNESDAY ♥

"Have faith in God," Jesus answered. "I tell you the truth, if anyone says to this mountain, 'Go, throw yourself into the sea,' and does not doubt in his heart but believes that what he says will happen, it will be done for him. Therefore I tell you, whatever you ask for in prayer, believe that you have received it, and it will be yours. And when you stand praying, if you hold anything against anyone, forgive him, so that your Father in heaven may forgive you your sins."
Mark 11:22-26

This is another one of my favorite scriptures. The Lord gave me this scripture very early in my stand twelve years ago.

Every time I read it, I get excited. **We need to pray with BELIEVING, FAITH-FILLED HEARTS.** That is the kind of prayer that moves mountains! Jesus was using the term "mountain" figuratively. My mountain twelve years ago was the "mountain of divorce." Your mountain could be adultery, separation, alcohol, drugs, physical or verbal abuse. Whatever mountain that is blocking your pathway, the prayer of faith can remove it.

Faith comes from looking at God and not at your circumstances. God gives us faith as we walk with Him. Pick up your cross and follow Him. Be obedient in following and doing what the Lord tells you to do daily.

The Lord showed us there were other conditions that must be met. Do not doubt, but believe and forgive others. Choose to forgive and the Lord will touch you and give you the spirit of forgiveness. Who do you need to forgive?

As you walk with God, your faith will grow, your confidence will increase, and your prayers will have power. Your mountain will be removed by our Lord Jesus Christ.

Search me, O God, and know my heart; test me and know my anxious thoughts. See if there is any offensive way in me, and lead me in the way everlasting. Psalm 139:23-24

As we talk to our Sovereign Lord today, may our heart's cry be that we are cleansed from all unrighteousness. May we repent of our ways that are not of the Lord and ask Him to remove our unclean ways, unclean thoughts, and wrong actions.

Who can discern his errors? Forgive my hidden faults. Keep your servant also from willful sins; may they not rule over me. Then will I be blameless, innocent of great transgression. May the words of my mouth and the meditation of my heart be pleasing in your sight, O Lord, my Rock and my Redeemer. Psalm 19:12-14

Today, ask the Lord to guide you in what you say, and in what you think, and in what you do.

We take captive every thought to make it obedient to Christ. 2 Corinthians 10:5

The Lord is near to all who call on him, to all who call on him in truth. Psalm 145:18

Great is our Lord and mighty in power; his understanding has no limit. Psalm 147:5

Have a great day with the Lord.

He is ALL you need!

Praise the Lord, O my soul. O Lord my God, you are very great; you are clothed with splendor and majesty. I will sing to the Lord all my life; I will sing praise to my God as long as I live. May my meditation be pleasing to him, as I rejoice in the Lord. Psalm 104:1,33-34

May you and I realize how great is our Lord! May we praise Him today regardless of our present circumstances and know He is in charge of our lives and our loved ones. **Praise the Lord for His greatness!**

Answer me when I call to you, O my righteous God. Give me relief from my distress; be merciful to me and hear my prayer. Psalm 4:1

We heard of a prodigal husband whose new job working with troubled youth requires that he take them to church each week. Let's pray that prodigals across the land might end up in a Bible preaching church this weekend and be convicted that the best place for them is not the pigpen of life, but right back at home.

Give thanks to the Lord, for he is good; his love endures forever. Let the redeemed of the Lord say this--those he redeemed from the hand of the foe, those he gathered from the lands, from east and west, from north and south. Then they cried out to the Lord in their trouble, and he delivered them from their distress. Let them give thanks to the Lord for his unfailing love and his wonderful deeds for men. Psalm 107:1-3,6,8

Have a great day thanking the Lord for all He is doing in your life!

Are you double-minded? What is double-mindedness? The dictionary says, "undecided, vascillating." The enemy tries to torment us with double-mindedness. You wake up and acknowledge that God is in control of your life and family. Then comes that message from your prodigal that upsets you. It might have been a long time since you've heard from the one you love, and the enemy plants thoughts in your mind about their lifestyle. Satan is trying to take away your faith by planting doubt, fear, and unbelief. **The enemy wants you to miss the miracle that God has for you.**

But when he asks, he must believe and not doubt, because he who doubts is like a wave of the sea, blown and tossed by the wind. That man should not think he will receive anything from the Lord; he is a double-minded man, unstable in all he does." James 1:6-8

That might sound strong when you read it for the first time. You ask God what you should do. He tells you, but you don't want to do it. Sounds normal, doesn't it?

You ask the Lord for scriptures and He gives them to you. Because the answer does not come during your time limit, you start doubting. The devil comes in and steals your FAITH and you do not even know when it happened! Does this sound familiar? If you hear answers to prayer, you get excited and you get hope and encouragement. If you get discouraged and depressed, and you do not CONTINUE TO BELIEVE what the Lord has told you--YOU BECOME DOUBLE-MINDED.

For they did not believe in God or trust in his deliverance. Psalm 78:22

In spite of this, you did not trust in the Lord your God, who went ahead of you on your journey, in fire by night and in a cloud by day, to search out places for you to camp and to show you the way you should go." Deuteronomy 1:32-33

You need to be SINGLE-MINDED. You have to be confident of what the Lord has shown you. He will not change His mind.

"Blessed is she who has believed that what the Lord has said to her will be accomplished!" Luke 1:45

What a promise! Pray against being double-minded. Ask the Lord to forgive you. Seek what He would have you do. Be around people who believe with you for your miracle. Stand firm and do not question how the Lord is going to do it.

"For nothing is impossible with God." Luke 1:37

Read Luke 1.

Luke chapter 1 tells of an angel that came to Zechariah and said, *"Your prayer has been heard."* Then Zechariah questioned God by asking, *"How can I be sure of this?"*

WE HOPE THAT ALL OF YOU
CAN BELIEVE IN GOD
AND THE POWER OF PRAYER!

Do not doubt but believe and have faith in God!

♥ SUNDAY ♥

Today as we go to church, let us all worship our Lord. May we praise Him for His greatness.

Great is the Lord and most worthy of praise; his greatness no one can fathom. Psalm 145:3

In our online Newsletter this weekend, we asked for weather reports from around the world. Cheryl, a stander from Michigan, reported to us what the weather was like in her city early Saturday morning: "Brilliant bright sun, 42 chilled degrees. A slight breeze of fresh, cold, north wind. Looking out my window, God had on display a beautiful colorfest! My burning bush is a brilliant red, my new sugar maple tree shouts out bright yellow. My neighbor's tree waves hello with a deep crimson red. **All around God says, 'Did you ever see such beautiful shades of color? Take your eyes off you and enjoy My color parade!!' "**

Today, may we let the Lord show us through His eyes all that He has given us. Let us see the world as our Lord sees it. Let us enjoy all that He has created for each of us. May you have a blessed Sunday!

Praise the Lord. How good it is to sing praises to our God, how pleasant and fitting to praise him. Psalm 147:1

Our Bible study group continues to study "Prayer." We discussed hindrances to our prayer life.

Read Psalm 66:18, Isaiah 59:2, and Hebrews 11:6.

Ask the Lord if there is anything blocking answers to your prayers. Do you have selfish motives for the restoration of your marriage? Would answers to your prayers bring glory to your Lord, advance His kingdom, or help His people?

" 'I will make them one nation in the land, on the mountains of Israel. There will be one king over all of them and they will never again be two nations or be divided into two kingdoms. They will no longer defile themselves with their idols and vile images or with any of their offenses, for I will save them from all their sinful backsliding, and I will cleanse them. They will be my people, and I will be their God.' " Ezekiel 37:22-23

Are your circumstances helping you grow spiritually? We often do not receive our answers to prayer for other reasons. Unanswered prayer may be due to prayerlessness. Are you praying fervently and regularly for your prodigal? Have you said, "I am not going to pray anymore and 'just let go and let God.' " That is what the enemy is wanting all of us to do for all our prayer requests. Instead, we need to learn Spiritual Warfare.

When Bob was gone, I earnestly prayed, fasted, and persisted in claiming scripture with Bob's name in them. A scripture that I like to pray for prodigals is Job 33:12-33. My prayer is that many of us would fast one meal every day for the restoration of marriages.

"Is not this the kind of fasting I have chosen: to loose the chains of injustice and untie the cords of the yoke, to set the oppressed free and break every yoke?" Isaiah 58:6

♥ TUESDAY ♥

Spring is a beautiful time of year here in Florida. We have a few cool days and many perfect days. In fact, many mornings I open the door just to check the temperature. Then I dress accordingly, a long or short sleeve dress.

How foolish I would be to find it to be cool outside and start complaining to Bob. To do that would be allowing the weather to affect my whole day.

The "temperature" of our stand for marriage restoration might change as often as our weather. Are you allowing that temperature to affect or ruin your entire day?

What should you wear on a "cool" marriage day? The same as you should be wearing on a "warm" marriage day: The Armor of God.

Put on the full armor of God so that you can take your stand against the devil's schemes. For our struggle is not against flesh and blood,...Therefore put on the full armor of God, so that when the day of evil comes, you may be able to stand your ground, and after you have done everything, to stand. Ephesians 6:11-13

As you get dressed for work, be sure to get dressed every day for the Lord; dress with the armor of God on you for any battles that may come against you.

"No weapon forged against you will prevail, and you will refute every tongue that accuses you." Isaiah 54:17

Remember, do not fear. *Because the one who is in you is greater than the one who is in the world. I John 4:4* Regardless of the temperature outside, remember who you are serving.

How awesome is the Lord Most High, the great King over all the earth. Psalm 47:2

Have a great day, regardless of the temperature!

♥ WEDNESDAY ♥

It's a question that you've probably asked about your marriage a thousand times over; "How could someone I thought was a Christian do this?"

That's the same question being asked in Paducah, Kentucky, where a young man shot and killed some of his classmates. Since Paducah is Bob's hometown, we've followed the news report on this horrible incident. The young suspect's pastor has known the suspect's family for most of his 31 years (things don't change much in Paducah). He married the parents. He taught the young man the Word of God. He also must be asking himself a thousand times over; "How could someone I thought was a Christian do this?"

That pastor provided one answer in yesterday's Paducah paper; "What he did was a devastating act. It was not the act of an atheist. **It was an act of a sinful Christian.**"

How can your spouse have fallen so low? Sin had entered their life.

It appears the people of Paducah are doing two things. They are leaning fully on the Lord during this crisis. They are also ready to forgive the young man that is involved.

May today be the day you deal with your problems like Bob's Kentucky cousins. Lean on the Lord for His help through your crisis and forgive.

"The thief comes only to steal and kill and destroy;..." John 10:10

"For if you forgive men when they sin against you, your heavenly Father will also forgive you. But if you do not forgive men their sins, your Father will not forgive your sins." Matthew 6:14-15

Therefore, if anyone is in Christ, he is a new creation; the old has gone, the new has come! All this is from God, who reconciled us to himself through Christ and gave us the ministry of reconciliation: that God was reconciling the world to himself in Christ, not counting men's sins against them. And he has committed to us the message of reconciliation. We are therefore Christ's ambassadors, as though God were making his appeal through us. We implore you on Christ's behalf: Be reconciled to God.
2 Corinthians 5:17-20

A few days ago we sent our Audio Newsletter tape to most of the people on our mailing list. Starting about tomorrow, we will receive many returned mail packages that cannot be delivered. We feel badly each time this happens, knowing that another stander did not receive the message we had for them.

Imagine with me that you're a passenger on a doomed flight about to crash. You're going to be in the Lord's presence in seconds. Would you be carrying any undelivered mail in your heart as that plane plunged toward the earth? Would your final thought on this side of eternity be, "I wish I told_____that_____?"

Would the Lord have you deliver your mail today, before it's too late?

Teach me to do your will, for you are my God; may your good Spirit lead me on level ground. Psalm 143:10.

May we be sensitive to the Holy Spirit's wooing to do His will in our lives.

Do you need to write or to call someone this week to say "I love you," or "Thank you," or "I am sorry," or "I forgive you?"

Seek the Lord today to find His will in your life.

♥ FRIDAY ♥

"I'm tired of hearing Romans 8:28 quoted to me by people with their spouse at home. Why don't they understand? My marriage has fallen apart."

The words of one person are no doubt the thoughts of many. How could anything good ever come out of the mess you have at home?

Anyone who watched television and saw that Paducah, Kentucky funeral, now has their answer. As we first heard about that horrible school shooting, no one had any idea of any good in that tragedy. Since then, the entire world witnessed half a dozen ministers proclaiming the Good News of Jesus Christ. We saw an invitation to come to Christ given live at the end of a two hour service. There is no way that anyone could have arranged for that television coverage to have been purchased. Not until eternity will we know what has happened in the hearts of many men.

Those parents must have heard Romans 8:28 over and over. The day of the funeral they saw that, yes, *"...all things work together for good to them that love God...."*

The Monday morning of your marriage has passed. I pray that you will STAND FIRM until your Friday afternoon is here. God is in it, so don't give up!

Read Romans 8:28-39.

Our Lord God is faithful to us and to OUR family. Just believe!

Great is the Lord and most worthy of praise; his greatness no one can fathom. Psalm 145:3

I truly can say, I am learning what the above scripture means. We were again privileged to share on the Trinity Broadcasting Network for thirty minutes about marriage restoration! What a miracle!

We received a telephone call to see if we were available to speak on TBN's South Florida Public Report program. We asked if the discussion had to be secular or could it be spiritual. They said it was up to the guest. As I sat in the studio, I recalled twelve years ago, in 1985, where I was so hard-hearted that I signed the final settlement papers in December. I hated Bob for what he had done to our family. The divorce became final in January, 1986.

Then in a few short weeks, the Lord touched me and spoke to my heart that I had given up on my Lord and on my one-flesh covenant husband. During the next two years as I cried and prayed for Bob, I kept thinking, "I hope we can help someone else not go through what we are going through."

"With man this is impossible, but not with God; all things are possible with God." Mark 10:27

In 1985, I never dreamed that we would be able to share the power of our awesome, mighty God, that our Lord hears our cries and heals our hurts, and that our Lord restores and rebuilds marriages on the solid rock of Jesus Christ--all on T.V.

May the Lord show you today that He will turn what the enemy meant for evil, to good.

They will speak of the glorious splendor of your majesty, and I will meditate on your wonderful works. They will tell of the power of your awesome works, and I will proclaim your great deeds. Psalm 145:5-6

Delight yourself in the Lord and he will give you the desires of your heart. Psalm 37:4

As we worship our Lord today, may we continue to **Commit, Trust, Delight,** and **Rest** in our Lord Jesus Christ.

Read Psalm 37.

The theme of this psalm is to trust in the Lord and wait patiently for Him to act.

As we read this psalm, we can see some principles we need to apply.

* Do not worry.
* Trust in the Lord.
* Delight in the Lord--not in your circumstances.
* Praise Him--He will change your attitude.
* Commit your way to the Lord--which means to turn everything over to the Lord completely--letting go and letting God change your circumstances.
* Be still before the Lord and wait patiently for Him.
* Trust Him to do what He has promised in His perfect timing.
* Believe in God that He knows, what is best for us.

Today, may we all start applying the principles in this psalm so that we can totally **Commit** our lives to His way, **Trust** Him completely, **Delight** in His presence and **Rest** in the Lord's timing and sovereign ways.

Have a blessed Sunday!

Sunday, in church, I saw Bob reading the words of a hymn. He asked Ed, who plays the piano for us each Monday night at Bible study, to play and sing it for the group. The words, Bob says, could be his confessional, as well as that of every returned prodigal. The hymn is titled "At Calvary."

At Calvary

Years I spent in vanity and pride,
Caring not my Lord was crucified,
Knowing not it was for me He died at Calvary.

By God's Word at last my sin I learned,
Then I trembled at the law I'd spurned,
Till my guilty soul imploring turned to Calvary.

Now I've giv'n to Jesus everything,
Now I gladly own Him as my King,
Now my raptured soul can only sing of Calvary.

Jesus told us in His Word that He will find our lost sheep.

"I am the good shepherd; I know my sheep and my sheep know me--just as the Father knows me and I know the Father--and I lay down my life for the sheep...My sheep listen to my voice; I know them, and they follow me." John 10:14-15,27

May you start today, not as a defeated victim of marriage problems, but as a child of the King, waiting and excited about serving Him. Bob and I pray today might be special for you!

♥ TUESDAY ♥

Let us then approach the throne of grace with confidence, so that we may receive mercy and find grace to help us in our time of need. Hebrews 4:16

This week's Bible study was "Listening To The Lord" as we pray. I suggested journaling and writing out prayers. Take time to listen, not talking, to be quiet, and to be still before the Lord. Listen for His soft voice.

"Be still, and know that I am God." Psalm 46:10

God does speak; through His Word, as a verse leaps off a page, through people, and through the Holy Spirit.

"But when he, the Spirit of truth, comes, he will guide you into all truth. He will not speak on his own; he will speak only what he hears, and he will tell you what is yet to come." John 16:13

God spoke to His people throughout the Old and New Testaments and He WILL speak to you.
This week, ask the Lord to speak to you.

I wait for you, O Lord; you will answer, O Lord my God. Psalm 38:15

Remember, **God DOES speak to His children!**

For the word of the Lord is right and true; he is faithful in all he does. For he spoke, and it came to be; he commanded, and it stood firm. The Lord foils the plans of the nations; he thwarts the purposes of the peoples. But the plans of the Lord stand firm forever, the purposes of his heart through all generations. Psalm 33:4, 9-11

Our Lord God is Creator, Lord, Savior, and Deliverer. He is worthy of our trust and praise. All God's words are right, true, and consistent. They can be trusted. The Bible is reliable and God does not lie, does not forget, does not change His words, and does not leave His promises unfulfilled.

Do you really believe what the Lord says in the Bible? **God says He hates divorce, shouldn't we?** God says that the man and woman became one flesh. Should we try to separate and divorce?

We can always trust the Bible because it contains the words of a holy, sovereign, trustworthy, and unchangeable God. Is there anyone else in this world that you could trust more? That knows more? We need to "Let Go and Let God" solve and work out our entire life. His way is the best way!

Every day we have a choice; His way or our way. Let's make a new commitment to "Follow His Way."

"For my thoughts are not your thoughts, neither are your ways my ways," declares the Lord. So is my word that goes out from my mouth: It will not return to me empty, but will accomplish what I desire and achieve the purpose for which I sent it." Isaiah 55:8, 11

God is Faithful!

♥ THURSDAY ♥

Hello, friend. I've asked my wife, Charlyne, if I might share with you.

I have a question. How much will you be praying for your spouse after the one you love comes home? The textbook answers might be, "every day" or "all the time." If, one year after your prodigal comes home, I asked how much you had been praying, could you still answer the same way?

It breaks our hearts when a returned spouse takes off again. Frequently, that has happened after a former stander stopped praying with the same intensity as was done while alone. Charlyne has said often that she will never stop praying for me. This week I saw the results of a praying wife.

I had driven a few blocks to the post office to get the mail. I then ventured across Highway One. On the way back while I was crossing the highway, an elderly gentleman ran a red light and broadsided my car. Although he hit me on the driver's door and my car was totaled, I didn't have a scratch on me. After everything was over and Charlyne had brought me home, we began to count the blessings. We've seen people killed at that same intersection when someone had run that light.

"Angels were around that car today," Charlyne reminded me. "Yes, Honey, I know they were. Thank God you are the kind of wife who summons them for me each day." I pray that your spouse will always be able to say the same about you.

"As for me, far be it from me that I should sin against the Lord by failing to pray for you. And I will teach you the way that is good and right." I Samuel 12:23

"No one will be able to stand up against you all the days of your life. As I was with Moses, so I will be with you; I will never leave you nor forsake you. Be strong and courageous, because you will lead these people to inherit the land I swore to their forefathers to give them. Be strong and very courageous. Be careful to obey all the law my servant Moses gave you; do not turn from it to the right or to the left, that you may be successful wherever you go. Do not let this Book of the Law depart from your mouth; meditate on it day and night, so that you may be careful to do everything written in it. Then you will be prosperous and successful. Have I not commanded you? Be strong and courageous. Do not be terrified; do not be discouraged, for the Lord your God will be with you wherever you go."
Joshua 1:5-9

Joshua had a new job which consisted of leading more than two million people into a strange new land and conquering it.

You have been given a job by your Lord to pray for your spouse and marriage. May this scripture encourage you to know that your Lord will never abandon you or fail to help you.

The Lord's message was to be strong and courageous, trusting and knowing the Lord is with you regardless of your circumstances.

Always obey God's principles, daily reading and studying His Word. Your God is faithful to His promises. He is always with you!

" 'Do not be afraid or discouraged because of this vast army. For the battle is not yours, but God's.' "
2 Chronicles 20:15

"Consecrate yourselves, for tomorrow the Lord will do amazing things among you." Joshua 3:5

Read Joshua 3.

Before entering the Promised Land, the Israelites were to perform a sanctification (purification) ceremony. God uses outward signs of uncleanness to illustrate man's inward uncleanness that comes as a result of sin. The sanctification ceremony pictured the importance of approaching God with a pure heart.

While our prodigals are gone, we are to consecrate and sanctify ourselves. Ask the Lord to reveal any uncleanness and sin in our heart. Confess and ask the Lord to give you a pure heart.

We want the Lord to do miracles as long as He does it our way. **Do you really believe in miracles? Miracles happen for God's glory.**

Joshua told the priest to take the ark of the covenant and cross over before the people. Joshua 3:6

If you are standing for a miracle, you need to change, cross the river of circumstances--get over your obstacle and stay committed. God didn't take you this far to leave you on the wrong side. Seek the Lord. You will find Him. You need to change from a life of doubt to a life of faith. **Cross over the river** of doubt into faith.

"This is how you will know that the living God is among you and that he will certainly drive out before you the Canaanites, ...set foot in the Jordan, its waters flowing downstream will be cut off and stand up in a heap." Joshua 3:10, 13

"Therefore say to them, 'This is what the Sovereign Lord says: None of my words will be delayed any longer; whatever I say will be fulfilled, declares the Sovereign Lord.' " Ezekiel 12:28

As you worship the Lord today, do not become discouraged if you should hear negative comments about standing and praying for your spouse. Believe what the Lord has said to you!

We go to church to be lifted up, but frequently we hear of standers getting hurt and defeated because of well-meaning friends saying discouraging comments. You are standing, interceding, and believing for a miracle in your marriage because of the Lord.

Most standers can tell us when the Lord revealed to them not to give up on their spouse or their marriage. Many tried not to pray, but the Lord continued to convict them of His plan and purpose.

As you share and talk to people in church, remember they did not receive the call, a word, a vision, or an assignment from the Lord, so they do not understand your burden or your calling. **Your Lord will accomplish what He has revealed to you in His timing.**

Read Daniel 10.

May we continue to pray for our men of God and our churches that they WILL NOT give up on marriages. **Pray that our churches WILL stand in the gap for all lost loved ones and believe in restoration and reconciliation.**

Have a blessed Sunday and don't give up!

Be on your guard; stand firm in the faith; be men of courage; be strong. Do everything in love. I Corinthians 16:13-14

May this scripture guide us this new week in what we believe, how we behave, and how we act as children of God.

Be on your guard against spiritual dangers.

Be self-controlled and alert. Your enemy the devil prowls around like a roaring lion looking for someone to devour. Resist him, standing firm in the faith, because you know that your brothers throughout the world are undergoing the same kind of sufferings. I Peter 5:8-9

Stand firm in your faith. Don't give up. Believe what the Lord can do.

It is for freedom that Christ has set us free. Stand firm, then, and do not let yourselves be burdened again by a yoke of slavery. Galatians 5:1

Whatever happens, conduct yourselves in a manner worthy of the gospel of Christ. Philippians 1:27

Be of courage and be strong; behave courageously. *Finally, be strong in the Lord and in his mighty power. Put on the full armor of God so that you can take your stand against the devil's schemes. Ephesians 6:10-11*

Do everything in kindness and love. *"A new command I give you: Love one another. As I have loved you, so you must love one another. By this all men will know that you are my disciples, if you love one another." John 13:34-35*

Now to him who is able to do immeasurably more than all we ask or imagine, according to his power that is at work within us. Ephesians 3:20

This is one of my many favorite scriptures. The reason is self explanatory. My Lord continues to amaze me, astonish me, shock me, thrill me, protect me, provide for me, and show me His mighty power. We serve an awesome, mighty God!

Tonight when I came home from work, Bob had a surprise on the web page. I had been asked by the Trinity Broadcasting Network to do a program on marriage. I had said, "Yes."

Bob did not go down with me that particular afternoon, as he did not feel well. As I was driving and praying, I was praising the Lord for the privilege to be able to share my testimony and to give hope and encouragement to other people who have marriage problems. They gave us a tape and we were given permission to put the program on our web page.

Tonight, Bob surprised me with that RealAudio program on the Internet site. What a miracle! Who am I?

Twelve years ago, my marriage was dead. I gave up on Bob and on God. Praise the Lord, the Lord knew my heart and gave me another chance.

Eighteen months ago, my husband was just recovering from a major stroke and brain surgery. See what the Lord has done!

Your Heavenly Father is planning and doing miracles in you and your loved ones' lives, also. **You may not see the fruit today, but keep praying and our Lord will provide the harvest.** Just imagine how the Lord will use you and your family in the future!

God is our refuge and strength, an ever-present help in trouble. Psalm 46:1

Do you feel like you can not handle any more problems? What is your largest problem? Remember that our Lord is always there to help you in your time of need. Give all your problems to the Lord.

The Lord Almighty is with us; the God of Jacob is our fortress. Psalm 46:7

He will provide you refuge, security, and peace. Believe in your Lord's power! He created the heavens and the earth! He said, *"Let there be light,"* (and there was light). Believe in His mighty power.

Read Psalm 91.

Have you had a bad day? Go to the Lord and pray. Ask the Lord to guide and direct each day. Ask for His wisdom. Learn to hear His soft voice. He will never forsake you.

"Be still, and know that I am God; "...The Lord Almighty is with us; the God of Jacob is our fortress. Psalm 46:10-11

"Do not let your hearts be troubled. Trust in God; trust also in me." John 14:1

Pray and believe God for your miracle!

"Do not grieve, for the joy of the Lord is your strength."
Nehemiah 8:10

Have you lost your joy? Throughout Jesus' teaching there is a theme of joy. Jesus wants you to have joy. The key to immeasurable joy is living in intimate contact with Christ, the source of all joy. Ultimate joy comes from Christ dwelling within us. One of the fruits of the Spirit is joy.

When the enemy attacks you, he is trying to steal your joy. Do not let the devil steal anything else from you. Satan wants you to react instead of praying. Have you lost your joy due to your circumstances?

Paul's attitude in prison is an important lesson we all can learn from; our inner attitudes do not have to depend on our outward circumstances.

About midnight Paul and Silas were praying and singing hymns to God, and the other prisoners were listening to them. Suddenly there was such a violent earthquake that the foundations of the prison were shaken. At once all the prison doors flew open, and everybody's chains came loose.
Acts 16:25-26

Consider it pure joy, my brothers, whenever you face trials of many kinds, because you know that the testing of your faith develops perseverance. Perseverance must finish its work so that you may be mature and complete, not lacking anything. James 1:2-4

Pray that your joy may come back regardless of your present circumstances.

Be joyful in hope, patient in affliction, faithful in prayer.
Romans 12:12

As obedient children, do not conform to the evil desires you had when you lived in ignorance. But just as he who called you is holy, so be holy in all you do; for it is written: "Be holy, because I am holy." I Peter 1:14-16

When you have been hurt, wounded, betrayed, and rejected, it often seems impossible to think or act as Jesus would. That is why Christianity is unique and special...it is not what we do, or say. It is what the Holy Spirit can do through us, when we ask Him to help us each day.

As we plan this weekend, may we start asking our Lord to change us to be more like Him. Then, and only then, will people see the true difference of why we are willing to pray and intercede for our loved ones. May we always point the reason we are standing and waiting for our prodigal to our Lord and Savior Jesus Christ.

There is a song that reminds us of this:

Take Time To Be Holy

*Take time to be holy,
Speak oft with thy Lord;
Abide in Him always
And feed on His Word.*

*Make friends of God's children,
Help those who are weak;
Forgetting in nothing
His blessing to seek.*

*Take time to be holy,
The world rushes on;
Much time spend in secret
With Jesus alone.*

By looking to Jesus,
Like Him thou shalt be;
Thy friends in thy conduct
His likeness shall see.

Take time to be holy,
Let Him be thy guide;
And run not before Him
Whatever betide.

In joy or in sorrow,
Still follow the Lord;
And, looking to Jesus
Still trust in His Word.

Take time to be holy,
Be calm in thy soul;
Each thought and each motive
Beneath His control.

Thus led by His Spirit,
To fountains of love;
Thou soon shalt be fitted
For service above.

Written by: William Dunn Longstaff

May we act and react as Jesus would. Ask the Holy Spirit to help us each moment. **Let's take time, by reading His Word and spending time, with Him, to be more like Him every day.**

Praise the Lord in singing every day!

♥ SATURDAY ♥

Who shall separate us from the love of Christ? Shall trouble or hardship or persecution or famine or nakedness or danger or sword? No, in all these things we are more than conquerors through him who loved us. For I am convinced that neither death nor life, neither angels nor demons, neither the present nor the future, nor any powers, neither height nor depth, nor anything else in all creation, will be able to separate us from the love of God that is in Christ Jesus our Lord. Romans 8:35, 37-39

Read Psalm 17.

My prayer for you this weekend is that no matter what has happened to you today or in the past, no matter where you are right now spiritually, you will NEVER forget God's love for you. Do not let your circumstances keep you from your Lord who died on the cross for you and for all of your loved ones. Bring all your problems and yourself to your Heavenly Father. He is waiting for you! **NOTHING can separate you from your Lord Jesus Christ and His love for you. He is with you in the midst of your worst storm. Call upon Him, right now!** He will meet you right where you are! With Him, we are conquerors in Christ!

I call on you, O God, for you will answer me; give ear to me and hear my prayer. Show the wonder of your great love, you who save by your right hand those who take refuge in you from their foes. Psalm 17:6-7

But thanks be to God! He gives us the victory through our Lord Jesus Christ. I Corinthians 15:57

The Lord hears and answers prayer.

He fulfills the desires of those who fear him; he hears their cry and saves them. My mouth will speak in praise of the Lord. Let every creature praise his holy name for ever and ever. Psalm 145:19, 21

Today as you worship the Lord at your church, may you truly forget all your problems and worship your Heavenly Father. He created you to have a personal relationship with Him. May you feel the presence of the Holy Spirit today.

I will lead the blind by ways they have not known, along unfamiliar paths I will guide them; I will turn the darkness into light before them and make the rough places smooth. These are the things I will do; I will not forsake them. Isaiah 42:16

Before you go to church, start praying for the services, the congregation, the pastor, and the musicians. Pray that the Lord will bring people from the north, the south, the east, and the west to hear the Good News. Pray that the lost will have their spiritual eyes and ears opened by the Lord and set free by the truth.

Each week the Lord uses circumstances that you and I could not even imagine to bring prodigals into His house. Please pray for prodigals who will find themselves, for whatever reason, in church today.

Lord, may they hear from You. Amen.

May the Lord have a mighty harvest today.

"I rejoiced with those who said to me, "Let us go to the house of the Lord." Psalm 122:1

Then he said to his disciples, "The harvest is plentiful but the workers are few. Ask the Lord of the harvest, therefore, to send out workers into his harvest field." Matthew 9:37

What is the most difficult time of the week for you as you stand for marriage restoration? Is it Saturday night or Sunday morning? Could it be Friday afternoons? If the time of the week hardest for you to face is Sunday evening/Monday morning, you are far from being alone.

Even though our mountains are small, we often have those mountaintop experiences of our stand on Sundays. There is often a joy and peace on Sunday that is beyond words. Then the sun sets. In a few hours, it will be business as usual. You will go from being with people who care on Sunday to a world that doesn't understand on Monday.

How excited would you be if you were leaving for a missionary assignment in a foreign nation on Monday morning. Well, you are, so get excited!

Bob has a quote written in the back of his Bible that says, **" God calls specific people to specific places for specific purposes."** Monday morning you will be in your mission field. You will see people this week that no one else can reach for Christ.

My prayer for you is that you might find true joy in serving God while you stand and pray for Him to make your marriage all He desires it to be. May today be not a "blue Monday" but a "blessed Monday."

"But you will receive power when the Holy Spirit comes on you; and you will be my witnesses in Jerusalem, and in all Judea and Samaria, and to the ends of the earth." Acts 1:8

Let the Lord fill your heart with joy.

"Nothing's changing in my marriage situation. Is God really at work?" How often we've each thought, or even said that statement. Day after day, everything remains the same.

> *He called out to them, "Friends, haven't you any fish?"*
> *"No," they answered.*
> *He said, "Throw your net on the right side of the boat and you will find some."*
> *When they did, they were unable to haul the net in because of the large number of fish. John 21:5-6*

The disciples had been fishing all night with no success. They remind me of spouses standing for marriage restoration with no success. Although they did not recognize Jesus, they did as He told and cast their nets in a different place with amazing results.

How long has it been since you asked Jesus where you should cast your nets for a restored marriage? The disciples were fishermen. They knew how to fish. Yet, it took the Lord's direction for them to get results.

Your stand might need a new direction from the Lord. He might be wanting you to cast your nets toward a more concentrated prayer life or fasting for your prodigal. Perhaps He will direct your nets toward giving up something for Him. I cannot imagine where all the Lord will have you to cast nets.

There are fish there. Prodigals do come home. I pray that today you might ask our Lord Jesus where you should be fishing.

Let your fishing bait be the fruit of the Spirit!

We constantly pray for you, that our God may count you worthy of his calling, and that by his power he may fulfill every good purpose of yours and every act prompted by your faith. We pray this so that the name of our Lord Jesus may be glorified in you, and you in him, according to the grace of our God and the Lord Jesus Christ.
2 Thessalonians 1:11-12

Paul wrote a letter to the church at Thessalonica to clear up a misunderstanding and to encourage this church to stand firm for Christ's truth. Paul wrote more than one prayer showing his true love and concern for his brothers and sisters in the Lord.

He wanted to stress that he was praying for the church people. His prayer was that God would count the people WORTHY of His calling on their lives. Paul wanted everyone to know it was by GOD'S POWER that they would fulfill every good PURPOSE in their lives, by their FAITH in their Lord Jesus Christ. "Worthy of His calling" means to "want" to do what is "right" and good or to ask "What would Jesus do?" This will all be accomplished only by God's wonderful grace, mercy, and love.

May you remember every day that the Lord has a plan and a purpose for your life and for your marriage. He is in control. Today, may we remember that our Lord is worthy of all our praise and that by His mighty power He will move those mountains of circumstances to accomplish His will.

Why does God work miracles today? So that we all will give Him all the Praise and Glory that He deserves.

You have a choice--believe or doubt. What is your choice? May we always choose to follow our Lord Jesus Christ and believe in His power to work miracles in our lives.

"....He has sent me to proclaim freedom for the prisoners and recovery of sight for the blind, to release the oppressed, to proclaim the year of the Lord's favor." Luke 4:18-19

Jesus was sent to die for each of us.

You see, at just the right time, when we were still powerless, Christ died for the ungodly. Romans 5:6

Your Lord was sent to save sinners like you and like your spouse. May you praise the Lord for all that He has done for you and for your family. **Recall your ungodliness before you were saved knowing that your spouse will also be touched!**

The Lord gave me a promise to claim. What is yours?

"I will heal their waywardness and love them freely, for my anger has turned away from them." Hosea 14:4

The Lord knows your spouse's heart and all their circumstances. He will heal and restore them at just the right time.

" 'The days are coming,' declares the Lord, 'when I will bring my people Israel and Judah back from captivity and restore them to the land I gave their forefathers to possess,' says the Lord." Jeremiah 30:3

Our Lord will do all that He needs to do to get your loved one's attention. May you never become weary praying for your lost prodigals to come home to their Lord and to their families. What would you want your spouse to do if the circumstances were reversed?

"....to be a covenant for the people and a light for the Gentiles, to open eyes that are blind, to free captives from prison and to release from the dungeon those who sit in darkness." Isaiah 42:6-7

Believe in the power of your Lord Jesus Christ. Your Lord touched Paul on the Damascus Road, so He can and will touch your spouse in His timing!

"....Then you will know that I am the Lord; those who hope in me will not be disappointed." Isaiah 49:23

GOD IS FAITHFUL.

HE WILL DO WHAT HE HAS PROMISED!

"Several nights ago, my husband called and told me he had repented to God and he shared with me what he'd been going through with the Lord. Then he asked me to forgive him and to take him back. Then he asked our kids for forgiveness....I would really like to encourage everyone to not give up! The end really does come! I haven't seen my husband for 16 months, nor even talked to him for almost a year when he was still being very cruel. I had no indication that this was happening. I know that the Lord kept trying to encourage me to hang on....It scares me now to think how close I was to give up when my miracle was right around the corner. So please don't give up!"

This is part of a letter we received today from another stander whose husband is coming home! What a praise report! Bob and I receive mail and emails each day for prayer requests. We hurt for all of you going through circumstances that we went through many years ago. When we receive a letter like we did today--it is worth all that we do! We are just praising the Lord!

In Genesis 41, Joseph was called to see Pharaoh about interpreting his dreams. One moment Joseph was in prison, and then suddenly Pharaoh said to Joseph, *"You shall be in charge of my palace, and all my people are to submit to your orders. Only with respect to the throne will I be greater than you." Genesis 41:40*

See what the Lord did suddenly! **I wish I could be with each of you to encourage you to never, never give up on your Lord God and your spouse!** I know how you hurt. You have fear that you are standing and your spouse will never come home! I know all the thoughts the enemy shoots at you. All we can say is, "Have faith, believe, and trust in your awesome mighty God you serve. He will never fail you, reject you, or hurt you."

After Joseph saw and talked to his brothers, he said, *"Don't be afraid. Am I in the place of God? You intended to harm me, but God intended it for good to accomplish what is now being done, the saving of many lives. So then, don't be afraid. I will provide for you and your children."* Genesis 50:19-21

Be encouraged and have a great weekend! Don't forget to pray in agreement for all prodigals "to come to their senses" this weekend!

May our prayers this weekend be *"I do believe; help me overcome my unbelief!" Mark 9:24*

THE LORD IS ALWAYS WITH YOU.

HE WILL SEE YOU THROUGH.

BE SURPRISED AT WHAT THE LORD CAN DO!

♥ SATURDAY ♥

Blessed is he whose help is the God of Jacob, whose hope is in the Lord his God, the Maker of heaven and earth, the sea, and everything in them--the Lord, who remains faithful forever. Psalm 146:5-6

Let's read Psalm 146 today knowing that all our help comes from our powerful, sovereign Lord.

May we all agree together, to pray that our Lord will touch each prodigal's heart this weekend to repent and turn from their wrongdoings.

The Lord sets prisoners free, the Lord gives sight to the blind, the Lord lifts up those who are bowed down, the Lord loves the righteous. Psalm 146:7-8

Pray that the Lord who heals, Jehovah-rapha, will touch and heal your prodigal's heart; taking the heart of stone and making it a heart of flesh. May we continue to remember the power of prayer.

"I tell you the truth, whatever you bind on earth will be bound in heaven, and whatever you loose on earth will be loosed in heaven. Again, I tell you that if two of you on earth agree about anything you ask for, it will be done for you by my Father in heaven. For where two or three come together in my name, there am I with them." Matthew 18:18-20

May this weekend be a new beginning in many of our prodigals' lives! Let's pray!

TRUST AND BELIEVE.

Praise the Lord. I will extol the Lord with all my heart in the council of the upright and in the assembly. Great are the works of the Lord; they are pondered by all who delight in them. Glorious and majestic are his deeds, and his righteousness endures forever." Psalm 111:1-3

Let's praise the Lord for who He is! As we worship our mighty Lord, may we remember the price our Lord paid at Calvary. May all believers unite in prayer this Sunday, knowing they can freely approach God's throne through prayer and have God in their lives through the Holy Spirit.

Read Psalm 111.

The works of his hands are faithful and just; all his precepts are trustworthy. They are steadfast for ever and ever, done in faithfulness and uprightness. Psalm 111:7-8

May our prayer today be that ALL of our prodigals will truly fear the Lord and be obedient to His will and His way.

The fear of the Lord is the beginning of wisdom. Psalm 111:10

Have a great day worshipping and praising our Lord.

I often state that Bob came home due to my praying and claiming scriptures with his name in them. Frequently we receive letters asking which scriptures I used to pray for Bob. There are many favorites. I love to write out prayers with scriptures in them.

This week may we cry out to our Lord that our spouse will listen and be obedient to the Great Counselor, Deliverer, and Savior.

I call on You, O God, for You will answer me; give ear to me and hear my prayer. It is God who arms me with strength and makes my way perfect. Forgive my hidden faults and keep me from willful sins; may they not rule over me. I praise You that You say all of us who once were far away have been brought near through the blood of Christ. My prayer, Lord, is that my spouse and loved ones will repent and be baptized in the name of Jesus Christ for the forgiveness of their sins. My prayer is that my loved ones and I will put off our old selves, which is being corrupted by its deceitful desires; to be made new in the attitude of our minds; and to put on our new selves, created to be like God in true righteousness and holiness. You said You will go and heal them. With Man this is impossible, but not with God; all things are possible with God. Praise be to the Lord forever! Amen and Amen.

Scriptures taken from: Psalm 17:6, Psalm 18:32, Psalm 19:12-13, Ephesians 2:13, Acts 2:38, Ephesians 4:22-24, Matthew 8:7, Mark 10:27, and Psalm 89:52.

May you feel the presence of the Lord with you each and every day this week!

♥ TUESDAY ♥

Monday night at Bible study, one of the scriptures we studied was **Matthew 14:22-33.** There we read:

"Lord, if it's you," Peter replied, "tell me to come to you on the water."
"Come," he said.
Then Peter got out of the boat, walked on the water and came toward Jesus. But when he saw the wind, he was afraid and, beginning to sink, cried out, "Lord, save me!"
Immediately Jesus reached out his hand and caught him. "You of little faith," he said, "why did you doubt?" Matthew 14:28-31

That same day Peter had participated with Jesus in the feeding of the five thousand and now in His walk on the lake. That's when the natural man in Peter kicked in. He began to sink and Jesus reached out His hand and saved him.

We know of hundreds who are "walking on the water" through separation and divorce. Some are in court today. Others are unemployed. Medical problems and car trouble are burdens for others. Jesus has called, "Come," and they are standing for marriage restoration, praying for the spouse who walked out on them.

I want to remind you, on this Tuesday, **that when we take our eyes off Jesus, we will sink.** The One who has called you to "Come" has not changed His call. I pray that today when the natural circumstances make you want to give up on that prodigal, you'll keep your eyes on Jesus.

But Jesus immediately said to them: "Take courage! It is I. Don't be afraid." Matthew 14:27

I wish you were here in our living room tonight to share my heart. I am very sad thinking about our spouses and family members. I went to see a very close friend, the wife of our printer, who is in ICU.

Norman found Marian barely breathing early Monday morning. They did CPR and rushed her to the hospital. They have diagnosed a terminal disease. She is breathing by a ventilator. Today, I was able to talk and pray with her.

I looked in that hospital room, crying, seeing a saintly, Godly woman lying there, saying to her husband and family, "Let me go, I am ready to meet my Lord." Family members were all by the bed praying for a miracle, but knowing that if she died we all would be rejoicing for her meeting her Lord.

How sad it is to think of your spouse lying in another bed, a bed of sin, fighting for his or her life. How unfortunate it is that friends and family members are not around to pray for this lost loved one. Friends and family say it is better for the spouse and family to get on with their life. Everyone will be better without them. What a devil's lie.

No one said words like that to the hurting and grieving spouse or family in ICU today. We were all hurting and praying for a miracle for this family. There is one adult child who is away from the Lord. Friends are praying that he will come to his senses and recommit his life to his Lord and Savior.

Oh, may we never forget to visualize our spouse fighting for their life. **May we pray that our Great Physician will touch and heal their spiritually dead heart.**

May we always remember to never give up on our spouses regardless of their physical or spiritual state. Visualize the one you love fighting for their life in ICU.

Pray for our Lord to restore your spouse completely. Never give up on your Lord or your spouse!

♥ THURSDAY ♥

Two women lay dying. One deep inside a prison in Texas, strapped to a gurney. The other in a hospital in Florida. One had been found guilty of two brutal murders. The other had lived her life for the Lord. Both knew Jesus, their Savior. By earthly time, they met Him face to face within hours of each other. Which one was welcomed into the kingdom of God? Both heard the welcome summons, *"'Well done, good and faithful servant!'"* *Matthew 25:23*

What does this have to do with troubled marriages? The one you love is living in sin. They have been acting as if there is no right or wrong. Your spouse may act as if there is no consequence to their sin. The Bible says there IS consequence to sin.

We will all die one day and face our Lord Jesus Christ. *Another book was opened, which is the book of life. The dead were judged according to what they had done as recorded in the books. Revelation 20:12*

Read Matthew 20:1-16.

This parable is not about rewards but about salvation. It is a strong teaching about grace, God's generosity. We see God's gracious acceptance of the sinner, who was despised and possibly an outcast, who has now turned to our Lord for forgiveness. *"But many who are first will be last, and the last first." Mark 10:31*

Let us use these two women, who both knew the Lord and when they died as examples of what the Lord can do in a sinner's life, regardless of what they have done previously.

Your Lord God loves your spouse just as much as He does these two women. **He will use many circumstances in life to bring the one you love back to the Lord and to a waiting family.** May these two women's testimonies encourage us to continue to persevere and intercede for our lost loved ones.

"With man this is impossible, but not with God; all things are possible with God." Mark 10:27

In John 11:41 we read one of the prayers of Jesus.

So they took away the stone. Then Jesus looked up and said, "Father, I thank you that you have heard me. I knew that you always hear me, but I said this for the benefit of the people standing here, that they may believe that you sent me."

Verse 43 tells us that *Jesus called in a loud voice, "Lazarus come out!"* We know the rest of this beautiful story.

Are you waiting for Jesus to call your seemingly dead marriage to life? Why is it taking so long? That might have been the exact question asked by Martha and Mary. Their brother had been sick. Jesus did not come. Their brother died. Still Jesus was not there. If anyone ever had a reason to give up, it was those women.

Re-read that prayer. Jesus prayed, *"...for the benefit of the people standing here..."* When Jesus prayed and then called Lazarus out, time did not matter. He could have been dead four days or four years. **When Jesus brings your dead marriage back to life, time will not matter. You could have been standing for four days or four years. Time will not matter. What does matter is your not giving up--no matter what happens!**

DEAD MARRIAGE, COME OUT!

'....O my people, I am going to open your graves and bring you up from them; I will bring you back to the land of Israel.' Ezekiel 37:12b

GOD WILL RESTORE YOUR MARRIAGE!

Israel said to Joseph, "I never expected to see your face again, and now God has allowed me to see your children too. " Genesis 48:11

What a powerful scripture! Israel thought Joseph was dead, but, as he was dying, He gave God the praise and glory for bringing home his son as well as his grandchildren!

When we talk about restoration many think of Joseph, who had his family restored after many years of circumstances.

Today, let us look at Jacob (Israel), the father. Jacob's story is told in Genesis chapters 25-50. Joseph was thought dead by his father, due to what his brothers had told him when they came home. Jacob (Israel) went into mourning for his son.

Right now you may be in mourning for your marriage. Eventually, God's plan allowed Jacob to regain not only his son, but his grandchildren as well. May you always remember your circumstances are never so bad that they are beyond God's help! Jacob regained his son. **May you always remember the powerful God you serve every day wants to reconcile and rebuild your marriage.**

You need to never despair or give up because you belong to a loving God. **You do not know how He will bring your trials and tribulations out of a seemingly hopeless situation, but He is able.**

Do you believe? Israel never expected to see Joseph again. See what the Lord did! He can also do this for you and your family.

Your marriage seems dead. Your spouse says he will never come home. May you remember to believe only what the Lord says. Israel had his children and grandchildren restored as a family. May you never give up regardless of your circumstances!

Every day our Lord is orchestrating events into each of your lives to bring you closer to Him. I am amazed and just praise His Holy Name for what He does for each of us every day. **He will never give up on any of His children!** Doesn't that just sound like a parent?

TRUST GOD TO WORK

ALL OF YOUR CIRCUMSTANCES OUT

BOTH FOR YOUR GOOD AND HIS GLORY!

"For God so loved the world that he gave his one and only Son, that whoever believes in him shall not perish but have eternal life." John 3:16

Today, may we all continue to pray for our lost loved ones. Yesterday we attended the funeral of a close friend. She was a Proverbs 31 woman, a prayer warrior and a soul winner. Testimonies at the service showed her deep concern for everyone's spiritual condition. May we all be concerned and pray for all sinners who do not know the Lord.

Bob and I pray every weekend that the Lord will have a victorious Sunday throughout the land saving many lost souls headed toward hell. None of us knows the future, so we all need to be ready to meet our Lord. That is one of the many reasons we pray earnestly for all prodigals. May you pray with us today for a large harvest.

"Repent and be baptized, every one of you, in the name of Jesus Christ for the forgiveness of your sins. And you will receive the gift of the Holy Spirit. The promise is for you and your children and for all who are far off--for all whom the Lord our God will call." Acts 2:38-39

What a promise! May our prayer be that your spouse and loved ones will repent of their sins, "turning from their sin." "To turn from sin" means changing the direction of your life from selfishness and rebellion against God's laws. You turn to Christ, depending on Him for forgiveness, mercy, guidance, and purpose. Have you made that commitment? If not, ask for forgiveness of your sins, then pray for Jesus Christ to come into your life as Lord and Savior. You will never be the same! Have a great day worshipping your Lord!

Jesus said to Simon Peter, "Simon son of John, do you truly love me more than these?" "Yes, Lord," he said, "you know that I love you." Jesus said, "Feed my lambs." Again Jesus said, "Simon son of John, do you truly love me?" He answered, "Yes Lord, you know that I love you." Jesus said, "Take care of my sheep." The third time he said to him, "Simon son of John, do you love me?" Peter was hurt because Jesus asked him the third time, "Do you love me?" He said, "Lord, you know all things; you know that I love you." Jesus said, "Feed my sheep." John 21:15-17

As we read this scripture, may we think about what Jesus is really asking Peter and us. Peter had denied Jesus three times. **Have you ever denied your Lord in your actions, in your behavior, or in words that you speak?** Peter realized how he had failed his Lord after the rooster crowed. Peter told Jesus he would lay down his life for Him and then he denied Him three different times! Then Peter wept bitterly.

Let's examine ourselves today. **Do we say to the Lord how much we love Him, but then we are not willing to follow His will and His way for the restoration of our marriage?** Do we cry out to our Lord and say things that we do not really want to do?

It is often easy to say you love someone, but the real test is your willingness to serve that person or to serve Jesus. Peter had repented. Jesus asked Peter to commit his life to Him and Trust Him. Has Jesus asked you these questions? Is He asking you, "Do you love me?"

What is your answer? Do you really love Jesus? Are you willing to follow Him? What does He want you to do? Is He asking you to sacrifice for your spouse? Has He asked you to obey and trust Him with love, joy and gladness?

May we always remember that Jesus loved us so much He died for you, for me, and for all our loved ones. May we this week show the Lord how much we love Him. May we show Him we are willing to follow Him all the way!

♥ TUESDAY ♥

"You did not choose me, but I chose you and appointed you to go and bear fruit--fruit that will last. Then the Father will give you whatever you ask in my name. This is my command: Love each other." John 15:16-17

The Lord has chosen you! He loves you so much He died for you! He wants each of us to bear fruit.

Read John 15:1-17.

"If you remain in me and my words remain in you, ask whatever you wish, and it will be given to you. This is to my Father's glory, that you bear much fruit, showing yourselves to be my disciples." John 15:7-8

Fruit is not limited to soul winning. We see prayer, joy, and love are mentioned as fruits. **Read Galatians 5:22-24** for more fruit qualities that affect your Christian character, such as: peace, patience, kindness, goodness, faithfulness, gentleness, and self-control.

As you stand for marriage restoration, let's ask the Lord to make you more like Him. You need to allow the Holy Spirit to lead your daily life. Live each day controlled and guided by the Holy Spirit, then as family and friends see you, they will see that you are different. You will react differently--your goal is to react as Jesus would.

Let the Lord change you from the inside out each and every day. Let us show God's love and joy so that we will be a magnet for our Lord Jesus Christ. In God's timing, our spouses will see the Lord in us and come to their senses.

"My command is this: Love each other as I have loved you. Greater love has no one than this, that he lay down his life for his friends." John 15:12-13

♥ 63 ♥

I have hidden your word in my heart that I might not sin against you. Praise be to you, O Lord; teach me your decrees. Psalm 119:11-12

I challenge you today, to hunger and thirst for the Word of God.

Read Psalm 119.

May we remember to read God's word for truth and direction in our lives. We need to always have the word in our hearts to help us through our trials and tribulations.

Blessed are they whose ways are blameless, who walk according to the law of the Lord. Blessed are they who keep His statutes and seek him with all their heart. Psalm 119:1-2

Open my eyes that I may see wonderful things in your law. Psalm 119:18

Teach me, O Lord, to follow your decrees; then I will keep them to the end. Give me understanding, and I will keep your law and obey it with all my heart. Direct me in the path of your commands, for there I find delight. Psalm 119:33-35

Your word is a lamp to my feet and light for my path. Psalm 119:105

You are my refuge and my shield; I have put my hope in your word. Psalm 119:114

I call with all my heart; answer me, O Lord, and I will obey your decrees. I call out to you; save me and I will keep your statutes. I rise before dawn and cry for help; I have put my hope in your word. Psalm 119:145-147

May we get excited about reading and learning the Word of God. We serve an awesome, mighty God. As you spend time with the Lord, may you hear His will and way for your marriage. Have a great day!

Do you believe your Lord's hand is powerful? Do you fear the Lord your God? Do you always obey the Lord regardless of what He wants you to do? We need to always remember the power of our awesome, mighty God.

Read Joshua 4.

And Joshua set up at Gilgal the twelve stones they had taken out of the Jordan. He said to the Israelites, "In the future when your descendants ask their fathers, 'What do these stones mean?' tell them, 'Israel crossed the Jordan on dry ground.' For the Lord your God dried up the Jordan before you until you had crossed over. The Lord your God did to the Jordan just what he had done to the Red Sea when he dried it up before us until we had crossed over. He did this so that all the peoples of the earth might know that the hand of the Lord is powerful and so that you might always fear the Lord your God." Joshua 4:20-24

God asked Joshua to build a memorial. God wanted to remind His people to always remember to put their focus on God. This would remind them He was going to guide them daily throughout their lives. If they needed a miracle, the stones would remind them of the miracles their family members had seen in the past and the power of their God.

Do you have time daily to focus on God's Word and time to seek His will and way for your life?

You are making a memorial in your home by standing for your marriage. Do you have traditions, special dates or special places that have a memory and a story--to show the power of prayer and a miracle in your life? Do your children know how you got saved? Do you share answers to prayers showing them your Lord's faithfulness?

As you stand for restoration, reconciliation, and rebuilding of your marriage, may you teach your children continually why you are praying and waiting for your spouse to come home. Share with your children the importance of the person regardless of their present behavior.

I will sing of the Lord's great love forever; with my mouth I will make your faithfulness known through all generations. Psalm 89:1

GOD'S LOVE IS ETERNAL.

GOD'S WORD IS ETERNAL.

GOD'S PROMISES ARE ETERNAL.

♥ FRIDAY ♥

Are you ready to give up? Do you feel no one understands what you are going through? Do you have circumstances that seem overwhelming? Do your finances seem impossible? Does everyone around you think you are crazy or not adjusting to your separation or divorce?

"In my distress I called to the Lord, and he answered me. From the depths of the grave I called for help, and you listened to my cry." Jonah 2:2

You need to cry out to your Lord. He hears your cries when everything looks hopeless.

May the God of hope fill you with all joy and peace as you trust in him so that you may overflow with hope by the power of the Holy Spirit. Romans 15:13

Give all your problems to God. Trust in Him. He will fill you with a joy and peace that is beyond understanding. Obey the Lord and He will provide for your every need. Today give all your worries, problems and concerns to the Lord. Leave them at His feet.

Trust in the Lord with all your heart and lean not on your own understanding; in all your ways acknowledge him, and he will make your paths straight. Proverbs 3:5-6

LET GOD GUIDE YOU IN ALL YOU DO.

In a vision a man imagined God, watching him as he tried to live the Christian life. Time after time, he tried to follow Christ and blundered. God said to those around him, "I am tired of forgiving him. He'll never change." Some of those in Heaven suggested to God what He should do; give up, find someone else to love, and stop allowing Himself to be hurt. Then the Lord spoke, *"Yea, I have loved you with an everlasting love." Jeremiah 31:3*

May we use our Lord Jesus Christ as an example, for His unconditional love for each of us to love our unlovable spouses at this present time. May we use His perseverance to speak love to our spouses or to our enemies.

May the Lord direct your hearts into God's love and Christ's perseverance. 2 Thessalonians 3:5

The world tells us to use tough love. That means, "If you don't do right, then I will do wrong." I am so glad that God loves me with an unconditional love and not with the tough love I often deserve.

"If you love those who love you, what reward will you get? Are not even the tax collectors doing that?" Matthew 5:46

But God demonstrates his own love for us in this: While we were still sinners, Christ died for us. Romans 5:8

This weekend may you seek the Lord for His will and His way regarding your marriage and your spouse's life. Do not take polls or surveys to find out the answer. Ask the Lord to show you whether you are to love your spouse with "tough love" or "unconditional love."

Are the scriptures coming alive to you? My deepest desire is that today your prayer will be to the Lord, "Speak to me, Lord; I want to hear from You." My desire is that you daily commune with your Heavenly Father.

Let the morning bring me word of your unfailing love, for I have put my trust in you. Show me the way I should go, for to you I lift up my soul. Psalm 143:8

As you go and worship the Lord today, ask Him to speak to you in a special way. Get up early and start each day with reading scriptures. Listen to praise music as you worship your Lord.

Tell Him your deepest fears, your concerns, and your needs. He is waiting for us to cry out to Him for our needs. He will direct your every step, if you will ask Him for His directions and His way.

You will weep no more. How gracious he will be when you cry for help. As soon as he hears, he will answer you. Although the Lord gives you the bread of adversity and the water of affliction, your teachers will be hidden no more; with your own eyes you will see them. Whether you turn to the right or to the left, your ears will hear a voice behind you, saying, "This is the way; walk in it." Isaiah 30:19-21

The Lord has allowed these circumstances, so ask Him what He wants you to do. Confess any sins, ask the Lord to speak to you this Sunday through the scriptures, sit waiting and expecting Him to speak to you. He will guide and direct you in ways you will have never thought possible.

Listen and hear my voice; pay attention and hear what I say. Isaiah 28:23

As our Lord teaches us His ways, are you learning? *The heart of the discerning acquires knowledge; the ears of the wise seek it out. Proverbs 18:15*

May our prayer this week be, "Lord, teach me more of what you want me to change and do in my own life."

Jesus went throughout Galilee, teaching in their synagogues, preaching the good news of the kingdom, and healing every disease and sickness among the people. Matthew 4:23

Jesus' ministry consisted of TEACHING people, PREACHING, showing His concern for people's commitment, and HEALING their sicknesses, showing His concern for wholeness.

Do you really believe in the power of your Lord? Do you know He can show you areas you need to change to be more Christ-like? Our Lord's way of living usually contradicts the world's way. May we apply the Biblical standards in our life and be more like Jesus every day.

"Blessed are those who hunger and thirst for righteousness, for they will be filled." Matthew 5:6

May we continue to seek the Lord this week. **May we apply the principles and teachings of our Lord Jesus Christ in a new and more determined way.**

"Therefore everyone who hears these words of mine and puts them into practice is like a wise man who built his house on the rock." Matthew 7:24

Let us focus our attention on ourselves and let the Lord work on our spouses!

♥ TUESDAY ♥

Blessed is he whose transgressions are forgiven, whose sins are covered. Blessed is the man whose sin the Lord does not count against him and in whose spirit is no deceit. Psalm 32:1-2

Read Psalm 32.

This psalm expresses the joy of forgiveness. The forgiveness of our sins brings true joy. Only when we ask God to forgive us of our sins will He give us real happiness and relief from our guilt.

May we praise the Lord today for our salvation. Praise the Lord for the forgiveness of our sins. Are you angry, jealous, or bitter? Do you have any unforgiveness? If you do, you need to repent and ask forgiveness of your sins. Do not let ANY sin block your relationship with your Lord. Do not let ANY sin block answers to your prayers.

May we continue to pray that ALL prodigals today will confess and ask for forgiveness of their sins.

Then I acknowledged my sin to you and did not cover up my iniquity. I said, "I will confess my transgressions to the Lord"--and you forgave the guilt of my sin. Psalm 32:5

Our Lord wants to direct our pathway and show us the best way we should go. Our Lord is wanting, waiting, and willing to guide each of us with love and wisdom. If we and our prodigals do not obey the Lord, He will use discipline to get our attention. So, let all of us seek the Lord.

Read Psalm 32:10.

Many are the woes of the wicked, but the Lord's unfailing love surrounds the man who trusts in him. Psalm 32:10

This is what the Lord says: "Restrain your voice from weeping and your eyes from tears, for your work will be rewarded, declares the Lord. "THEY WILL RETURN FROM THE LAND OF THE ENEMY. So there is HOPE for your future," declares the Lord." Jeremiah 31:16-17 (emphasis mine)

Let us believe in our Lord God's mighty power. He loves our spouses and children more than we do. He sees your tears on your pillow as you go to bed alone or while you are driving to and from work with all your circumstances coming against you. If you will be obedient to His will and His way, He will answer your prayers. Just hold on!

"But seek first his kingdom and his righteousness, and all these things will be given to you as well." Matthew 6:33

Throughout the Bible we see God restoring His people. He wants us to never forget how much He loves His children. **May we always remember that our Lord God is calling His lost sheep throughout every day many different ways.** May our prodigals be led to pray this next scripture.

"Restore me, and I will return, because you are the Lord my God. After I strayed, I repented; after I came to understand, I beat my breast. I was ashamed and humiliated because I bore the disgrace of my youth." Jeremiah 31:18-19

Our Lord God is wanting to have every sinner repent every day. Imagine how grieved He must be as they continue to sin and rebel. The Good News is that He has made promises to His people, may we never forget to claim the promises of God.

"The time is coming," declares the Lord, "when I will make a new covenant with the house of Israel and with the house of Judah. This is the covenant I will make with the house of Israel after that time," declares the Lord. "I will put my law in their minds and write it on their hearts. I will be their God, and they will be my people. For I will forgive their wickedness and will remember their sins no more."
Jeremiah 31:31, 33, 34

MAY WE ALWAYS REMEMBER

THE PRECIOUS PROMISES OF GOD!

♥ THURSDAY ♥

Let us then approach the throne of grace with confidence, so that we may receive mercy and find grace to help us in our time of need." Hebrews 4:16

How are you approaching the throne of grace? Is it with confidence and boldness, or with weakness, timidness, or unworthiness? And The meaning of confidence in the dictionary is: "Firm belief; trust; reliance; the fact of being or feeling certain; assurance." **May every time we pray to our Lord Jesus Christ, we pray with confidence knowing for certain that He hears our prayers and cries!** Remind yourself of the meaning of confidence--FIRM BELIEF AND TRUST! The enemy is constantly stealing from us the assurance of who we are in Christ! We are children of the King! We are victorious in Christ!

We need to believe and trust so we may RECEIVE mercy and FIND grace in our time of need. The Greek for "help" in that verse is "boetheia." Strong's Concordance explains that boetheia was a chain or a rope used for frapping a vessel and it derives its meaning from "boethos"- a succourer or helper. To frap a boat one must wrap ropes or cables around it in order to strengthen, support, and steady it. In those days, if a ship was caught in a storm or in a weakened condition for one reason or another, they would pass ropes or chains under and around the vessel and tighten them to secure the ship and to help hold it together in the midst of the storm.

Many of you may feel like you cannot make it. You are like a ship out at sea being tossed to and fro ready to fall apart and sink! The enemy is constantly saying, "You will never make it!"

May we remember this scripture to KNOW FOR CERTAIN, that our Lord and Savior is ready to rescue us, to hold us together, to guide us out of the storm and put us safely on shore. Your God is faithful and He will take care of you!

It is his power that holds everything together.
Colossians 1:17 TLB

♥ FRIDAY ♥

One of the most common questions I am asked is, "What should I do when my spouse is being so angry, hateful, or unlovable?" Many people suggest "tough love" or consequences to their behavior. I try to ask myself, "What would Jesus do?"

Do not repay anyone evil for evil. Be careful to do what is right in the eyes of everybody. If it is possible, as far as it depends on you, live a peace with everyone.
Romans 12:17-18

Read Romans 12:9-21.

I had asked the Lord many similar questions years ago. I kept being directed by the Lord to love Bob unconditionally. I asked the Lord to put His love in me so that I could love Bob the way He loved Bob. He put an unconditional love in me for Bob. The Lord is so good! The only way we can do this is by the renewing of our mind. (Romans 12:1-2)

Now that we are Christians, Jesus wants us to act differently. We are to be more like Jesus every day. When we read the Gospels we see that, Jesus used many examples. He was practical. He told us to be more Christ-like, to be sanctified, and to yield to holiness. We are to die to the sinful nature or the characteristics of the carnal flesh. Jesus said, *"Pick up your cross and follow me."*

As believers, we must resist the temptation to retaliate when our spouses wound us. Instead, we need to promote our sanctification by doing good to those who do evil to us. As the world looks at us, may they see Jesus. **Then in God's timing; He starts to restore, He starts to reconcile, and He starts to rebuild our marriages.**

Do not be overcome by evil, but overcome evil with good."
Romans 12:21

Be patient then, brothers, until the Lord's coming. See how the farmer WAITS for the land to YIELD its valuable crop and how PATIENT he is for the autumn and spring rains. You too, be PATIENT and STAND FIRM, because the Lord's coming is near. James 5:7-8 (emphasis mine)

Tonight, I just want to praise the Lord for His faithfulness. In the recent weeks, we have received letters and emails from standers who are going through the daily circumstances of hurt, of pain, of divorce papers, and of divorce court proceedings. Regardless of each of the circumstances, you mention your pain, but you also say you are seeking and crying out to your Lord. Many of you have been given the opportunity to share from your heart when the circumstances permit. PTL!

I just want to encourage all of you to be like the farmer; WAIT, BE PATIENT, AND STAND FIRM. You will see the Lord YIELD His VALUABLE crop if you will only PERSEVERE.

As you know, we consider blessed those who have persevered. You have heard of Job's perseverance and have seen what the Lord finally brought about. The Lord is full of compassion and mercy. James 5:11

Continue to show your spouse unconditional love regardless of their behavior. Act and think like the farmer. We, as standers, need to WAIT, BE PATIENT, AND STAND FIRM for a very valuable crop--your spouse and your family members' salvations for generations to come!

Let's pray for all prodigals and standers this weekend.

Today as we worship our Lord, may we feel the presence of the Lord with us in a very special way. As you stand for the rebuilding and restoration of your marriage, may you pray for a revival in all of our churches and in our land.

May we be like Elijah and show others through our faith that your God is able to do anything! As you may feel lonely, remember God is always there. He will never let you be put to shame.

I sought the Lord, and he answered me; he delivered me from all my fears. Those who look to him are radiant; their faces are never covered with shame. Psalm 34:4-5

Read I Kings 18.

Elijah was used by the Lord to show which God was more powerful. Which God are you serving daily? May you choose whom you will serve. Stop wavering and BELIEVE!

Elijah went before the people and said, "How long will you waver between two opinions? If the Lord is God, follow him; but if Baal is God, follow him." I Kings 18:21

May we earnestly pray daily for all prodigals to SEE and KNOW the truth. That each one will be set free from the enemy of deception, lust and disobedience. May each prodigal cry out to their Heavenly Father.

"O Lord, God of Abraham, Isaac and Israel, let it be known today that you are God in Israel and that I am your servant and have done all these things at your command. Answer me, O Lord, answer me, so these people will know that you, O Lord, are God, and that you are turning their hearts back again." Then the fire of the Lord fell and burned up the sacrifice, the wood, the stones and the soil, and also licked up the water in the trench. When all the people saw this, they fell prostrate and cried, "The Lord--he is God! The Lord--he is God!" I Kings 18:36-39

Do you really believe that God does heal people from their sinful ways?

In the March, 1998, <u>Charisma and Christian Life</u> magazine, there is an article titled, "Why Do Christians Shoot Their Wounded?" It's a very good article and gives us the opportunity to re-evaluate our reaction to our church body and leaders who fall into sin. It states, "People need to know that God desires and is able to forgive, heal and restore anyone." Many Christians, due to the world's standards, have become more worldly than scripture regarding Christians who have fallen into sin.

Do we believe in mercy and grace or do we harbor unforgiveness? Do we feel that our prodigals never knew the Lord or do we recognize that they fell into satan's trap? Do we love sinners as Jesus does?

Read John 8:1-11.

"...If any one of you is without sin, let him be the first to throw a stone at her." Again he stooped down and wrote on the ground. John 8:7-8

What was Jesus' judgment against the woman's adultery? **Jesus emphasized His compassion and forgiveness. What are you feeling about your prodigal?** Is that a sin?

May this story remind each of us of our own sinful nature. Jesus did not condemn the woman accused of adultery, but He did not ignore or condone her sinful behavior. He told her to leave her life of sin.

May we continue to pray that all prodigals will listen to the Holy Spirit's conviction of their sinfulness; confessing and repenting, changing their heart. With God's help, all prodigals can accept Christ's forgiveness and stop all wrong-doing! PTL! Keep praying!

"Do not be afraid. Stand firm and you will see the deliverance the Lord will bring you today. The Egyptians you see today you will never see again. The Lord will fight for you; you need only to be still." Exodus 14:13-14

Read Exodus 14 and 15.

Does your situation seem hopeless? Do you feel trapped by circumstances that seem impossible to change? That is how the Israelites felt when they were being chased by the Egyptians between mountains and the sea.

Did the Israelites trust God? No, they grumbled and complained. What lack of faith, after they had just been delivered by God from Egypt.

Where are you? Are you grumbling and complaining to family and friends about your spouse? Do you really believe in your God's faithfulness? When the enemy starts throwing circumstances at you; *"Do not be afraid. Stand firm and you will see the deliverance the Lord will bring you today."* We do not have any power, but your God does!

May we always remind ourselves, when it is getting darker, to cry out to your Lord, for His great wisdom and protection from the enemy. He will deliver you! *"The Lord will fight for you; you need only to be still."*

Call upon the Lord to rescue you. Look up and see what the Lord will do for you and your family!

"Who among the gods is like you, O Lord? Who is like you--majestic in holiness, awesome in glory, working wonders?" Exodus 15:11

We serve an awesome, mighty God! He will take care of you!

So Joshua fought the Amalekites as Moses had ordered, and Moses, Aaron and Hur went to the top of the hill. As long as Moses held up his hands, the Israelites were winning, but whenever he lowered his hands, the Amalekites were winning. When Moses' hands grew tired, they took a stone and put it under him and he sat on it. Aaron and Hur held his hands up--one on one side, one on the other--so that his hands remained steady till sunset. So Joshua overcame the Amalekite army with the sword." Exodus 17:10-13

Bob and I want to be your Aaron and Hur, helping and holding up your arms so that you can continue to praise your Lord and defeat the enemy. We do not want you to get weary or tired of the battle that you are in at the present time.

Then the Lord said to Moses, "Write this on a scroll as something to be remembered and make sure that Joshua hears it." Exodus 17:14

As I was praying, "standing," and believing for a miracle in my marriage, I wrote down many of my thoughts in a journal. After Bob came home, we reread my prayers and cries to the Lord. One evening, Bob went and got his diary and my journals, comparing dates and my heartfelt cries to my Lord. It was unbelievable. Time and again were answers to my prayers, as Bob noted in his diary to call me or spend time with our children. God does answer prayers!

Keep a journal. In the future, you will be able to show your children and grandchildren the history of your faith walk with your Lord.

Moses built an altar and called it The Lord is my Banner. He said, "For hands were lifted up to the throne of the Lord." Exodus 17:15-16

"Stand still, and see the salvation of the Lord." Exodus 14:13

Dear children, let us not love with words or tongue but with actions and in truth. I John 3:18

This is a scripture for and about standers. This scripture shows how many of you need to be willing to lay down your life for others. Your action is showing others how much you really love your spouse and other loved ones.

Now that you know these things, you will be blessed if you do them. John 13:17

Jesus showed us His love for us by laying down His life for all of us, when we did nothing to deserve His free gift of eternal life.

Whatever you have learned or received or heard from me, or seen in me--put it into practice. And the God of peace will be with you. Philippians 4:9

As you hear or read the Word of God, know that you must also put it into practice. How easy it is to hear a sermon and forget what the pastor said. How easy it is to read the Bible, but never apply it to our personal life and live differently. We need to allow the word of God to lead us to obedience following the example our Lord Jesus Christ gave us. Let us apply the precepts the Word of God has given us.

It is very easy to say we love our spouses unconditionally. What do our words and actions say? May we ask our Lord Jesus Christ to help our tongue and feet to align with our deepest heart's desire.

...Do you want evidence that faith without deeds is useless? Was not our ancestor Abraham considered righteous for what he did when he offered his son Isaac on the altar? You see that his faith and his actions were working together, and his faith was made complete by what he did. And the scripture was fulfilled that says, "Abraham believed God, and it was credited to him as righteousness," and he was called God's friend. You see that a person is justified by what he does and not by faith alone. James 2:20-24

REMEMBER TO PRAISE THE LORD

WHEN HE ANSWERS YOUR PRAYERS.

♥ FRIDAY ♥

Are you in the midst of a circumstance that seems impossible?

Read Daniel 6.

Daniel was one of three administrators for King Darius. Daniel was a very good example for the Lord, as he worked very efficiently and was more responsible than the other administrators.

Because of his good work habits, Daniel made enemies. The jealous officials couldn't find anything about Daniel to criticize so they decided to find something wrong with his God.

The men had the king issue a new decree that no one could pray to any god or man except the king, for the next thirty days or they would be thrown into the lion's den.

Do you feel like your situation is impossible? There is no hope or answer? Are you ready to give up on God? I know, I did twelve years ago. I did not know or trust my God that He would, or could, do anything to change all of my circumstances. **I did not believe or know His power, His greatness, or how awesome He truly is!**

Would you deny or stop praying to your Lord? Daniel had to make a decision.

Now when Daniel learned that the decree had been published, he went home to his upstairs room where the windows opened toward Jerusalem. Three times a day he got down on his knees and prayed, giving thanks to his God, just as he had done before. Daniel 6:10

The other men told the king what Daniel had been doing, so the king had no choice but to throw Daniel into the lion's den.

The king said to Daniel, "May your God, whom you serve continually, rescue you!" Daniel 6:16

Are you an example, wherever you may be, that your God is able to handle any circumstance? **May Daniel's prayer life motivate us to take more time to talk with our Lord daily.**

The next morning, the king went to the den to see if Daniel's God had saved him.

Daniel answered, *"My God sent his angel, and he shut the mouths of the lions. They have not hurt me, because I was found innocent in his sight." Daniel 6:22*

Believe that your God is able and will deliver you from any impossible situation. Are you willing to trust Him? How big is your God? My God is able to do anything!

"With man this is impossible, but not with God; all things are possible with God." Mark 10:27

WE SERVE AN AWESOME GOD!

♥ SATURDAY ♥

This weekend stand firm on the promises of our God. Our Lord sees your spouse's sinfulness, but He also knows the future. He knows the plans and the future of your family. May we all stand in agreement in what our Lord God is doing right now for all the prodigals. Your God sees and He also heals!

"I was enraged by his sinful greed; I punished him, and hid my face in anger, yet he kept on in his willful ways. I have seen his ways, but I WILL heal him; I WILL guide him and restore comfort to him, creating praise on the lips of the mourners in Israel. Peace, peace, to those far and near," says the Lord. "And I WILL HEAL them." Isaiah 57:17-19 (emphasis mine)

May we always remember our Lord sees and knows our heart. He hears our cries and our burdens. He hates divorce. He wants our children to have mothers and fathers raising their children together. He created it that way. Keep looking up and don't give up!

He will deliver even one who is not innocent, who will be delivered through the cleanness of your hands. Job 22:30

May we all pray this prayer for all prodigals who are away from their Lord Jesus Christ. May this Sunday be a Victory Day for our Lord Jesus Christ, bringing home His children from the far country.

May we all pray in agreement that our God is able to open all prodigals' spiritual eyes and ears to see the Truth and the Truth shall set them free!

We pray that God will grant _____ and all prodigals repentance, leading them to a knowledge of the truth, and that they will come to their senses and escape from the trap of the devil, who has taken them captive to do his will. Thank you, Father that you have rescued our prodigals from the dominion of darkness and brought them into the kingdom of the Son he loves, in whom we have redemption, the forgiveness of their sins. We pray that each prodigal will count themselves dead to sin but alive to God in Christ Jesus. We pray that they will not let sin reign in their mortal body so they will not obey its evil desires. Our prayer is that _____ and each prodigal will offer them- selves to God, as those who have been brought from death to life, and offer their body to Him as instruments of righteousness. Search _____ and each prodigal, O God, and know their heart; test them and know their anxious thoughts. See if there is any offensive way in them, and lead them in the way everlasting. Set _____ and each prodigal free from their prison, so that each one may praise your name. Lord, cleanse _____ and all prodigals from all their impurities and from all their idols. Give them a new heart and put a new spirit in them. Remove from them their heart of stone and give them a heart of flesh. Lord, you said you would save them from all their uncleanness. Thank you, Lord, that you will save them from all their sinful backsliding, and You will cleanse them. Lord, You said, on the day You cleanse _____ and our prodigals from all their sins, You will resettle their towns and the ruins will be rebuilt. All will know that I, the Lord, have rebuilt what was destroyed and have replanted what was desolate. I, the Lord have spoken, and I will do it. They will be my people, and I will be their God. I will give them singleness of heart and action, so that they will always fear me for their own good and the good of their children after them. Praise the Lord. Give thanks to the Lord, for He is good; His love endures forever. Amen.

Scriptures taken from: 2 Timothy 2:25-26, Colossians 1:13-14, Romans 6:11-13, Psalm 139:23-24, Psalm 142:7, Ezekiel 36:25-26,29,33,36, Ezekiel 37:23, Jeremiah 32:38, Psalm 106:1

At our local Bible study we completed a seven-week study of Ephesians. It was exciting and encouraging to read verse-by-verse out loud Chapter 6 verses 10 through 20. That passage in most Bibles is titled, "The Armor of God."

I encourage you to read those verses out loud. Yes, we all know what they say, but do we really KNOW the message being given to us? Verse 12 is key:

For our struggle is not against flesh and blood, but against the rulers, against the authorities, against the powers of this dark world and against the spiritual forces of evil in the heavenly realms.

The KJV Bible translates the word as "wrestle." The word implies throwing or swinging. The verse presents a personal foe with face-to-face and hand-to-hand conflict to the finish--a life and death struggle.

I need to remind you of two facts that Bob and I have said over and over. First, your spouse is not your enemy, regardless of what is happening. Second, the battle is the Lord's. No one ever won a war without knowing the enemy. Satan is the enemy who is trying to destroy your home.

I don't want "Charlyne Cares" to become a television review, but one episode of Sunday night's <u>Touched By An Angel</u> program gave the secular world (as well as many standers) a visual reminder of the battle being described in Ephesians 6. The story told about two young men, blinded and deceived by the world, who had beaten an innocent man. The only witness said that he had seen a third person in the car--satan.

The next time you have opposition, try to picture satan being right there. Bob said that if you meet satan head-on, it only means that you're not going in his direction.

Now, who is your enemy? What will you do?

Put on the full armor of God so that you can take your stand against the devil's schemes. Ephesians 6:11

♥ TUESDAY ♥

Read Romans 8:12-38.

If God is for us, who can be against us? Romans 8:31

Are you living by faith? Do you really believe that living by faith actually works? Oh, I remember as if it were yesterday when my heart's cry was, "Lord, I have no faith, help me, I am alone, I am sinking, what do I do now?" Don't look at tomorrow, let's just look at today. The Lord wants you to walk by faith, one moment, one day at a time. You may be at a crossroad in your spiritual walk. Who do you really serve?

I am not ashamed of the gospel, because it is the POWER OF GOD FOR THE SALVATION OF EVERYONE WHO BELIEVES: first for the Jew, then for the Gentile. For in the gospel a righteousness from God is revealed, a righteousness that is by faith from first to last, just as it is written: "The righteous will live by faith." Romans 1:16-17 (emphasis mine)

So do not throw away your confidence; it will be richly rewarded. You need to persevere so that when you have done the will of God, you will receive what He has promised. Hebrews 10:35-36

Do not become defeated or discouraged by doubt, fear, or the present pain you are in now. During this trial of tribulation, may you always remember whom you serve, the God of salvation. The God who sent His Son to die on the cross for all sinners. That includes you, your spouse, and your loved ones.

Now hold on, endure for a season, and persevere by faith. Faith means resting in what Christ has done for us in the past, but it also means trusting Him for WHAT HE WILL DO FOR US IN THE PRESENT AND IN THE FUTURE.

"The thief comes only to steal and kill and destroy; I have come that they may have life, and have it to the full." John 10:10

You are in a spiritual battle? Do you believe that? A thief came into your home and took your spouse hostage. Your spouse is spiritually blinded and deceived.

Read Mark 9:14-29.

"But if you can do anything, take pity on us and help us." " 'If you can?' " said Jesus. "Everything is possible for him who believes." Immediately the boy's father exclaimed, "I do believe; help me overcome my unbelief!" Mark 9:22-24

This is a story about a father seeking that his child be delivered and healed from an evil spirit. When the disciples tried to help the child, they could not. The father wanted his child helped and healed more than anything--he came and sought Jesus, just as you are seeking Jesus now for the healing of your marriage.

What that father said, is how many of you feel, "But if you can do anything, take pity on us and help us." Is that not your cry today? Faith and confidence are gifts from God. **The father longed for stronger faith and God granted his request, not because he saw mature faith, but because He honored his desire for growth.** Tell your Heavenly Father, "I do believe; HELP ME OVERCOME MY UNBELIEF!"

Later when the disciples asked Jesus why they could not cast the evil spirit out, Jesus answered, *"This kind can come out only by prayer and fasting."* May this teach us that at times during our stand, we may need to not only pray, but fast.

During my stand, at different times, the Lord would nudge me to fast for Bob. I would see Bob so blinded and so disobedient to God's will and way. I would cry out to my Lord, "What else can I do?" Then the Lord took me to the scriptures and showed me the power of fasting.

"Is not this the kind of fasting I have chosen: to loose the chains of injustice and untie the cords of the yoke, to set the oppressed free and break every yoke?" Isaiah 58:6

"I tell you the truth, whatever you bind on earth will be bound in heaven, and whatever you loose on earth will be loosed in heaven. Again, I tell you that if two of you on earth agree about anything you ask for, it will be done for you by my Father in heaven. For where two or three come together in my name, there am I with them." Matthew 18:18-20

If you do not know about spiritual warfare, ask the Lord to start teaching you.

Finally, be strong in the Lord and in his mighty power. Put on the full armor of God so that you take your stand against the devil's schemes. For our struggle is not against flesh and blood, but against the rulers, against the authorities, against the powers of this dark world and against the spiritual forces of evil in the heavenly realms. Ephesians 6:10-12

Let's join the Lord's army! He has won the war!

♥ THURSDAY ♥

When are the "Last Days?" After you read **2 Timothy 3:1-5**, you would think we are in the last days right now. Are we Christians any different? Are we afraid to be different? Today, let's examine ourselves and see if we really want to be different.

But mark this: There will be terrible times in the last days. People will be lovers of themselves, lovers of money, boastful, proud, abusive, disobedient to their parents, ungrateful, unholy, without love, unforgiving, slanderous, without self-control, brutal, not lovers of the good, treacherous, rash, conceited, lovers of pleasure rather than lovers of God--having a form of godliness but denying its power. Have nothing to do with them. 2 Timothy 3:1-5

After I read this scripture for a devotion this morning, I became deeply distressed. I asked Bob, "Where are we headed?" I have prayed today for our nation to repent. We need a revival for our land. May we cry out to our Lord for Him to touch and heal our nation.

People will be lovers of themselves, lovers of money.
2 Timothy 3:2

That sounds like our nation today. We care more about ourselves and how we look than we care for our children. Many fathers and mothers put their careers ahead of their children. Some parents would rather exercise and keep in shape than go to their children's baseball or hockey games. Many people think success and money can buy their happiness. We know it cannot.

People who want to get rich fall into temptation and a trap and into many foolish and harmful desires that plunge men into ruin and destruction. For the love of money is a root of all kinds of evil. Some people, eager for money, have wandered from the faith and pierced themselves with many griefs. I Timothy 6:9-10

May we always remember to love our family and people more than money. Love God's work more than money because money does not buy happiness.

SEEK GOD'S WILL FOR YOUR FAMILY.

Lovers of pleasure rather than lovers of God--having a form of godliness but denying its power. 2 Timothy 3:4-5

There are so many in the world today who do not believe in the power of your Lord Jesus Christ. Do you believe in the power of your Lord?

There are many people who care more about the pleasures of life than putting their Lord God first. Many people today profess being Christians, but do they know Jesus as Lord and Savior of their life?

We need to lay our life at the feet of Jesus and say, "Your way is the only way."

May we remind ourselves every day that our Lord Jesus Christ has power.

"Ah, Sovereign Lord, you have made the heavens and the earth by your great power and outstretched arm. Nothing is too hard for you." Jeremiah 32:17

May we not be like the people in the "Last Days" and have a hint of Christianity, but have no power.

Trust does not come easy. It wasn't easy for Moses to believe that he and his people would escape Egypt. It isn't easy for us to believe that God can fulfill His "impossible promises" for us today as He did in the Bible.

I did not believe in God's power 12 years ago, so I divorced Bob. Since then, God has revealed His power to me in so many ways through so many circumstances.

You are the God who performs miracles; you display your power among the peoples. Psalm 77:14

May you be different. Get to know and ask the Lord to reveal His power to you. He is the same yesterday, today and forever. He will be with you regardless of your circumstances. Do not be afraid, believe in the power of your God.

"Be strong and courageous. Do not be afraid or discouraged because of the king of Assyria and the vast army with him for there is a greater power with us than with him. With him is only the arm of the flesh, but with us is the Lord our God to help us and to fight our battles."
2 Chronicles 32:7-8

THE LORD IS YOUR STRENGTH

IN THE MIDST OF YOUR BATTLES.

PLACE YOUR TRUST IN HIM.

Therefore, as God's chosen people, holy and dearly loved, clothe yourselves with compassion, kindness, humility, gentleness and patience. Bear with each other and forgive whatever grievances you may have against one another. Forgive as the Lord forgave you. And over all these virtues put on love, which binds them all together in perfect unity. Colossians 3:12-14

This weekend, may this scripture be your prayer. May you remember that God created you. He loves you with an everlasting love. He has a plan and a purpose for your life. He will turn this crisis in your life to something great in the future. Like He did for Noah, David and Job, He will never fail you. Keep looking up at your Heavenly Father, waiting, persevering, and expecting a miracle in His timing.

This is what the Lord says--he who made a way through the sea, a path through the mighty waters, who drew out the chariots and horses, the army and reinforcements together, and they lay there, never to rise again, extinguished, snuffed out like a wick: "Forget the former things; do not dwell on the past. See, I am doing a new thing! Now it springs up; do you not perceive it? I am making a way in the desert and streams in the wasteland." Isaiah 43:16-19

May the Lord continue to give you compassion and grace to love your spouse who is living in their sinful nature and lifestyle. Examine your own heart and see if you are all that you should be. If you have allowed anger, bitterness, and unforgiveness to creep into your life, may you ask the Lord to forgive you.

May your spouse see the compassion, kindness, humility, gentleness and patience that you have in your heart, overflowing to them through the power of the Holy Spirit.

May you continue to forgive your spouse daily, so that you will not allow the enemy to bring up old garbage and sins that will ignite a fire at the inappropriate time. Let unconditional love pour over each of you, a love which will hold two people together in perfect unity as you and your spouse are "one-flesh." Love never fails!

Choose to be more like Jesus every day. Are you willing to be different this weekend?

LET'S BE MORE LIKE JESUS EVERY DAY!

For no matter how many promises God has made, they are "Yes" in Christ. And so through him the "Amen" is spoken by us to the glory of God. "Now it is God who makes both us and you stand firm in Christ. He anointed us, set his seal of ownership on us, and put his Spirit in our hearts as a deposit, guaranteeing what is to come.
2 Corinthians 1:20-22

Do you believe in the promises of God? I do! I did not several years ago, but the Lord showed me His power and His faithfulness to His Word. **So, stand firm on the promises of God!**
A beautiful song, by R. Kelso Carter, speaks of the faithfulness of God. The chorus says:

Standing on the Promises

Standing, standing,
Standing on the promises
Of God my Savior;

Standing, standing,
I'm standing on the
Promises of God.

Are you standing on the promises of God or are you afraid to believe?

So do not fear, for I am with you; do not be dismayed, for I am your God. I will strengthen you and help you; I will uphold you with my righteous right hand. Isaiah 41:10

Do not be afraid. Our God says, *"Fear not."* Trust your Lord with everything including your spouse and marriage.

When I am afraid, I will trust in you. In God, whose word I praise, in God I trust; I will not be afraid. What can mortal men do to me? Psalm 56:3-4

The Lord wants all of us to believe in His promises. He wants all sinners to come to know Him as Lord and Savior. Believe and stand on the promises of God.

The Lord is not slow in keeping his promise, as some understand slowness. He is patient with you, not wanting anyone to perish, but everyone to come to repentance. 2 Peter 3:9

Memorize this scripture! What a promise!

PUT YOUR TRUST IN GOD!

Don't worry! Do not be anxious!

Easy to say, but often hard to do! Well, this is the weekend before Thanksgiving. As a woman, I have more to do than hours to do everything I want to do! I am sure many of you can relate.

Read Matthew 6:25-34.

This is one of my special scriptures. At least two times in the past 12 years, the Lord gave me this scripture and then He moved a mountain of circumstances.

Many of you are dreading this Thanksgiving due to your marriage problems. Let's start planning for your dinner. Should you invite someone over to your house? Write your menu and get your grocery list started, or have you been invited over to someone else's house? Be sure to take one of your special dishes!

Let's stop worrying about why or where your spouse is going to be. Let's just keep praising and thanking the Lord for ALL THAT YOU DO HAVE RIGHT NOW.

"O you of little faith? So do not worry, saying, 'What shall we eat?' or 'What shall we drink?' or 'What shall we wear?'....But seek first his kindgom and his righteousness, and all these things will be given to you as well. Matthew 6:31,33

There is a song titled, "Tell It To Jesus." Today tell your Lord your concerns, then trust Him to answer and remove all of your anxieties. Have a great day planning your Thanksgiving! If you do not have plans yet, ask the Lord today what you are supposed to do!

♥ THANKSGIVING ♥

I believe in miracles. Do you? This afternoon, after a Thanksgiving feast at our church, several standers went to the ministry office to work for three hours mailing out our Audio Newsletter. We all thought before starting that it was going to take another evening of work. Many of them had already worked two evenings during the week doing the mass mailout to standers on our mailing list. Less than three hours later....it was done! PTL! We all were astonished and praised the Lord for His help. We then prayed for all the standers who are standing and believing for their marriage to be restored. We, also, prayed for each stander to have a special and blessed Thanksgiving.

Read Philippians 4:4-13, 19.

Our prayer is that each of you will look forward to this Thanksgiving. Yes, be thankful!

Rejoice in the Lord always. I will say it again: Rejoice!....Do not be anxious about anything, but in everything, by prayer and petition, with thanksgiving, present your requests to God. And the peace of God, which transcends all understanding, will guard your hearts and your minds in Christ Jesus. Philippians 4:4-7

Here are our instructions from Paul: Be joyful, don't worry about anything, just pray asking and thanking our God for all things. Then you will have a peace knowing that your God is in control of everything in your life.

Read this scripture every day this week. Don't worry about Thanksgiving. Tell the Lord your concerns and He will solve any problems, giving you a peace beyond understanding.

♥ THANKSGIVING ♥

As we prepare for Thanksgiving, let us also prepare to talk to our Father more. As we discussed in our recent Bible study class, let us examine our prayer time. I want to emphasize on the prayer pattern of A.C.T.S.

Today is A: ADORATION

Adoration sets the tone for the entire prayer. It reminds us of God's identity. God is faithful, righteous, just, merciful, gracious, willing to provide, attentive, unchanging, omnipotent, and omnipresent. Focus on God's greatness. Adoration purifies the one who is praying.

Our Lord God is worthy of ADORATION and WORSHIP. Do you approach God casually, or do you come as though you were invited before a king? A true worship experience is often a direct result of preparation for worship. Genuine worship results in submission and obedience to Jesus.

Read Psalms:8, 9, 19, 23, 46, 95, 100, 145-150.

Read Psalms to praise and worship your holy, awesome God. Let's start praising and worshiping our mighty Lord.

HE IS FAITHFUL IN ALL THAT HE DOES!

While Charlyne is getting ready for Thanksgiving, it might be a good time for me to remind you that Bob cares also. This week, my wife has had us look at our prayer life in view of A.C.TS. Yesterday, we saw A = Adoration. Today the word is (gulp) C = Confession.

We all have our favorite verses of *confession*, such as I John 1:9.

If we confess our sins, he is faithful and just and will forgive us our sins and purify us from all unrighteousness.

But, how does God really want us to confess? I admit to being guilty of, "Father, forgive me my sins and now here's a long list of things I need."

If I were to walk into the local police department and confess to robbing a bank, they would want details. How? Why did you do it? (That could be a tough one, Lord). Who helped? Did you harm anyone? (Lord, do I really need to confess that?) My bank robber confession would involve details. Does God expect any less from us?

There would be another part to the confession of Bob, the bank robber. At some point, the one who represented me would tell a judge and jury that I wasn't going to rob any more banks.

Confession involves repentance. Jesus Christ, the One who represents us, has told the Father that we have confessed and that we won't do it any more. May He help you and me to live that way.

May Thanksgiving be a special and blessed time for you.

♥ THANKSGIVING ♥

Give thanks to the Lord Almighty, for the Lord is good; his love endures forever. Jeremiah 33:11

Our prayer is that all of you have a blessed and thankful Thanksgiving. This Thanksgiving may have been the most difficult one for many of you. I pray as the Thanksgiving season is over and the Christmas season is just beginning, that we will search our hearts for things that we can be thankful for. Sit down by yourself and get a pencil and paper and start a list of the things that you can thank your Lord for today. You will be surprised, regardless of your present circumstances, that each of us has much to be thankful. Thank God for answered prayer, spiritual blessings, relational blessings, and material blessings.

Enter his gates with thanksgiving and his courts with praise; give thanks to Him and praise his name. Psalm 100:4

Many years ago, when we were having marriage problems, I was given a scripture which has become one of my favorites. May it be special for you today.

Be joyful always; pray continually; give thanks in all circumstances, for this is God's will for you in Christ Jesus. I Thessalonians 5:16-18

Let us not be like the nine men who had leprosy and were healed by Jesus who never thanked God, but be like the ONE who came back praising and thanking Jesus.

We give thanks to you, O God, we give thanks, for your Name is near; men tell of your wonderful deeds. Psalm 75:1

♥ CHRISTMAS ♥

I heard it for the first time this morning. As the radio was coming on, the words filled the room, "Joy To The World, The Lord Is Come." As I listened to the words that followed, I had to thank the Lord that He allows us to share His Good News with the entire world through Christmas music.

Then it hit me! So many people, even Christians, have such a difficult time during this time of year. The enemy must not think much of the music of Christmas being played everywhere. He must pull out ALL the stops to defeat us. When but December could you go shopping and hear music about Jesus being played overhead?

The shepherds watching their flock at night had a visitor who was also playing a tremendous song, praising the Lord!

Suddenly a great company of the heavenly host appeared with the angel, praising God and saying, "Glory to God in the highest, and on earth peace to men on whom his favor rests." Luke 2:14

As we all do our preparations for Christmas, may we also remember to pray continuously that one more Christmas carol or one memory might bring our prodigals to their senses to come home to their Lord and to their family for the holidays.

May we praise the Lord for this season and not let the enemy take away the true meaning of Christmas from each of our homes!

♥ CHRISTMAS ♥

Christmas is almost here!

Every year I suggest for us all to start reading the Gospels about the birth of our Lord Jesus Christ. The time is here again to start that tradition.

Today join me in reading Luke 1.

I prefer Luke to the other Gospels as I love to teach about Zechariah. He was a priest praying for a miracle; that his wife would have a child. An angel of the Lord appeared to him saying, *"Do not be afraid, Zechariah; your prayer has been heard." Luke 1:13*

What a comment! What encouragement to you and to me that our Lord hears our prayers.

Unfortunately, Zechariah did not believe the angel and said, *"How can I be sure of this? I am an old man and my wife is well along in years." The angel answered, "I am Gabriel. I stand in the presence of God, and I have been sent to speak to you and to tell you this good news. And now you will be silent and not able to speak until the day this happens, because you did not believe my words, which will come true at their proper time." Luke 1:18-20*

Do you believe in what the Lord has told or shown you regarding your marriage? Do not be like Zechariah and doubt what the Lord has told you. We need to always remember, "God's Word, God's promise will come true at the proper time!"

DO YOU BELIEVE? LORD, HELP THEIR UNBELIEF!

So do not throw away your confidence; it will be richly rewarded. You need to persevere so that when you have done the will of God, you will receive what he has promised. Hebrews 10:35-36

We received a note from a stander today praising the Lord as his wife asked him to come and celebrate Christmas with her and her daughter. PTL!

May we earnestly pray that many prodigals will be obedient to the Lord and come home to the Lord and to their families for Christmas!

Let us throw off everything that hinders and the sin that so easily entangles, and let us run with perseverance the race marked out for us. Hebrews 12:1

May we continue to have confidence, patience, and strength to "hold on" for God's best.

Perseverance reveals a genuine commitment. The rewards will be worth the effort.

As you know, we consider blessed those who have persevered. You have heard of Job's perseverance and have seen what the Lord finally brought about. The Lord is full of compassion and mercy. James 5:11

A young girl in Pennsylvania was traveling by train with her parents. She was terrified of the tunnels. Each time they entered one, she clung tightly to her dad. With eyes closed, she would not let go until her parents assured her they were out of the tunnel. Then she suddenly changed. As they entered the next tunnel she seemed thrilled, with her face pressed against the glass. Her mother asked her what made the difference. The little girl replied, "Now I know tunnels have light at both ends."

Bob and I know so many of you are going through the tunnels of life. All around, we hear and see others who appear so happy and talking about having a "Merry Christmas." Yet, all you see is a dark tunnel.

May today be the day that you remember that tunnels have light at both ends. Until you can see the light at the end of your tunnel, may you remember that you have a Heavenly Father to be with you in the darkest part of your tunnel.

Now may the Lord of peace himself give you peace at all times and in every way. 2 Thessalonians 3:16

What a way to start the day! Early Sunday morning, a stander called to report on a phone call she had just received from her husband. He had a question. Was his half of the closet empty? He was on the way home--right then. Praise the Lord!

We want to respect their privacy, but I can assure you of a few things. He has been gone from home for quite a while, and yes, their circumstances are as complicated as are yours. The enemy has thrown just about all he had at that wife during her stand for marriage restoration. Yes, she had her down days, but she always allowed the Lord to get her back on track.

Two weeks ago at Monday Bible study, we asked the Lord to bring prodigals home during this season of miracles. That stander has her miracle today.

Here is my question for you. Are you facing Christmas with the confident expectation that the Lord is at work in your situation? If that phone beside you rang RIGHT NOW and your spouse asked if half of the closet was empty, what would you say? Would you be like the prodigal's father, ready to welcome the one you love with open arms, or would you need to call a few friends to ask what you should do?

I pray that today you will be ready and open, in every way for all the Lord wants to do for your family. Let's pray for more prodigals to come home!

"I will search for the lost and bring back the strays...."
Ezekiel 34:16

Perhaps because it is part of a victory story of a marriage being restored, but we received more email about the prodigal's empty closet mentioned on Monday than from any other devotion that we've sent to you.

Monday, while reading your email, I began to reflect on our closet. It's the same one that I had half-emptied and readied for Bob. His suits, I could only see there by faith twelve years ago--now hang there. I went into our bedroom and looked inside the closet. It needs cleaning out. A blouse hangs on the door. There are shoes and clothes there I'll never wear again. Since Bob is now disabled, he doesn't wear many suits. Some of my things have crept into his side of the closet.

My bedroom closet could use cleaning. What about the closet of my heart? Have I allowed things to get in the way? I confess to you that I was not the perfect stander. There were times when the closet was ready for Bob, but my heart wasn't as neat and receptive.

Someone once said that Advent is the time when we oil the hinges to the door of our heart in preparation for the Lord's coming. I pray that each stander might use this Advent season to prepare for celebration of the birth of Jesus by cleaning the closet of the heart.

Therefore, rid yourselves of all malice and all deceit, hypocrisy, envy, and slander of every kind. I Peter 2:1

Father, I pray that you will help us to be ready, because prodigals do come home.
Amen

"Stop doubting and believe." John 20:27

I asked our weekly Bible study group a question, "Who are you like? Are you like Zechariah, like Mary, or like Joseph?" Today, let's look at Zechariah.

Every day each of us never knows what is going to happen that may change our life.

Read Luke 1:5-22.

Zechariah was chosen by God to do a special work for God. Zechariah and his wife had shared the pain of not having children.

During a trip to the temple in Jerusalem, Zechariah was chosen to be the priest who would enter the Holy Place to offer incense to God for the people. Suddenly, much to his surprise and terror, he found himself face to face with an angel. The angel's message was too good to be true.

Zechariah did not respond to the news of the coming Savior as much as he expressed DOUBTS about his own ability to father the child the angel promised him. As a result of Zechariah's doubt, God prevented Zechariah from speaking until the promise became reality.

Zechariah often becomes our hero for those times when we doubt God and yet are willing to obey. We learn from Zechariah that physical limitations do not limit God. God accomplishes His will, sometimes in unexpected ways.

May we learn NOT to ask the Lord the questions, "How can I be sure of this How can I be sure of my marriage being restored?" May we always remember, all the answers He gives, all the signs, and all the promises.

Never doubt God by having to see everything. May our prayer be, "Lord, increase my faith."

Each day, each hour, and each minute, we have a

choice of how we react or what we say to simple or difficult circumstances. We can respond like Zechariah or we can respond as Mary did. Continue to read Luke 1:46-56, and see how Mary truly praised the Lord for being chosen by Him.

May we remember that the Lord has chosen each of us to do a special assignment! May we all answer as Mary did!

MERRY CHRISTMAS

TO YOU AND YOUR FAMILY!

"Blessed is she who has believed that what the Lord has said to her will be accomplished." Luke 1:45

I asked our weekly Bible study group a question, "Who are you like? Are you like Zechariah, like Mary, or like Joseph?" Today, let's look at Mary.

Read Luke 1:26-56.

As we look at these special people in the Bible, may we compare our marriage standing to what each of these people were asked to do for the sake of many people and for generations to come.

Mary was chosen! Mary's life was quite satisfactory. She had recently become engaged to a carpenter, Joseph, and was anticipating married life. But, her life was about to change forever.

When the angel visited Mary, she did not doubt the message, but rather asked how the pregnancy would be possible. Gabriel told her the baby would be God's Son. Mary's answer was the one God waits in vain to hear from so many people...."I am the Lord's servant. May it be to me as you have said." Luke 1:38

Are you willing to be like Mary, chosen and appointed by God to have a special assignment? Mary was willing to be available to God. At the time the Lord called her, she had to prepare herself. She must have gone through many dark, lonely, and dreadful days, wondering how she was going to tell Joseph, her espoused. What would people say? What shame? Who would believe her? Isn't that often how you feel right now with your circumstances?

Often a person's character is revealed by his or her response to the unexpected. How would you rate yourself? God's plan often involves extraordinary events in ordinary people's lives.

Are you willing to be like Joseph and obey God regardless of the circumstances and ridicule that you may get from your family and friends? As you stand, pray and believe God for marriage restoration.

TRUST THE LORD!

"You intended to harm me, but God intended it for good to accomplish what is now being done, the saving of many lives." Genesis 50:20

PRAISE THE LORD

THIS CHRISTMAS SEASON

FOR THE GIFT OF HIS SON, CHRIST THE LORD!

....An angel of the Lord appeared to him in a dream and said, "Joseph son of David, do not be afraid to take Mary home as your wife, because what is conceived in her is from the Holy Spirit".... When Joseph woke up, he did what the angel of the Lord had commanded him and took Mary home as his wife. Matthew 1:20, 24

This week we have been thinking about, "Who are you like? Are you like Zechariah--doubting, like Mary--open to doing the Lord's will, or like Joseph? Today, let's look at Joseph.

Read Matthew 1:18-25.

Joseph will be the final person this week we want to compare to how we stand and pray for our families.

Joseph was a righteous man and did not want to publically expose Mary to shame and disgrace. Joseph was shocked and his heart was broken by this trial, but there was only one course left open for him. He would have to conclude the marriage--he could not marry her. He was prepared to do what was right, despite the pain he knew it would cause. Joseph decided he would put Mary away privately somewhere.

But, the Lord heard Joseph's cry and sent an angel to speak and direct Joseph's future. God had a plan and a purpose for Joseph that he could not even imagine. Joseph obeyed God. Joseph followed God's leading and was empowered to be Jesus' chosen earthly father!

"For I know the plans I have for you," declares the Lord, "plans to prosper you and not to harm you, plans to give you hope and a future." Jeremiah 29:11

God's ways are not your ways. God's timing is not your timing. We need to totally trust our Heavenly Father that He knows what is best for you and your family at this very moment.

Do you not know? Have you not heard? The Lord is the everlasting God, the Creator of the ends of the earth. He will not grow tired or weary, and his understanding no one can fathom. He gives strength to the weary and increases the power of the weak. Even youths grow tired and weary and young men stumble and fall; but those who hope in the Lord will renew their strength. They will soar on wings like eagles; they will run and not grow weary, they will walk and not be faint." Isaiah 40:28-31

This is the last weekend before Christmas. We all probably have a much longer list of things we need to do than we have time to complete.

As we finish preparing for Christmas, may we stop and make time for the Lord.

Many have become very tired and weary. Many are depressed and cannot wait until January 1. Where are you? Tell the Lord how you really feel. Ask Him to give you a new meaning of Christmas this year. May you make time this weekend to stop and prepare your hearts and minds for Christmas.

May you ask the Lord to renew your strength. If you feel like life is crashing all around you due to many circumstances, call on the Lord. He will give you hope, encouragement, and will renew your strength.

HE WILL MEET YOU RIGHT WHERE YOU ARE.

HE WILL NEVER FAIL YOU.

HAVE A GREAT DAY!

Have you ever noticed that women seem to be much busier than men as we prepare for Christmas? That is a blessing for me, because I get to share my heart with you again today.

I recently met a person who I had previously only communicated with by letter. Let me confess that I had envisioned a cool, distant person. What a blessing it was to discover that person was not at all like the letters I had received. The Lord used that experience to teach me.

Are you guilty of this same sin? Across the land are scores upon scores of people who have formed wrong opinions about someone they have never met. That Person is our Lord Jesus. They think they know Him--until they really meet Him.

Some feel their poverty comes from God. Then they meet Jesus, who owns it all. Others feel God made their marriage fall apart. Then they meet Jesus, the One who heals.

How about you? Do you know my Jesus? Many are so lonely at this time of the year, yet the Friend of Friends waits to be their companion.

The greatest Christmas gift is knowing Jesus. No, not knowing about Him, but knowing Him. That is my prayer for you today; that you would meet Jesus.

And I pray that you, being rooted and established in love, may have power, together with all the saints, to grasp how wide and long and high and deep is the love of Christ, and to know this love that surpasses knowledge--that you may be filled to the measure of all the fullness of God. Ephesians 3:17-19

...."*Do not be afraid. I bring you good news of great joy that will be for all the people.*" *Luke 2:10*

When Zechariah, Mary, Joseph, and the shepherds all saw the angel, each one was told, *"Do not be afraid."*

May I say to each of you this week, "Do not be afraid." At our weekly Bible study, that was my message this week.

Find time soon to read the promises in Luke 2:8-15 and Matthew 2:1-12.

Do not be afraid of your circumstances this week, or this coming year. Your Lord God is with you and He will never forsake you.

The shepherd and the Wise Men went to see, to find, and to follow the star that God used to announce the birth of His Son.

Are you willing to go and seek the Lord? Are you willing to worship your Lord? The Wise Men offered their very best. What are you offering your Lord? I pray that it is more than scraps.

The Lord wants you to remember the true meaning of Christmas. What are you going to be bringing to the Lord as a gift? Could it be a closer relationship with Him; sacrificing time to put Him first in your life?

Our prayer for you this Christmas is, "Do not be afraid." Follow the star that leads to Jesus. He has a plan and a purpose for you. Who do you choose to follow; His will and His way, or the world's way? He will never fail you!

♥ CHRISTMAS ♥

Twas the night before Christmas,
And all up and down the coast,
Not a creature was stirring,
Maybe a praying stander at most.

I was nestled all snug in my bed,
Visions of my prodigal danced in my head.
All of a sudden, there came such a boom,
Maybe a coconut hitting the Florida room.

I jumped out of bed and headed for the phone,
"Oh, God, please help me, I'm scared and alone."
Before I could dial, I heard the sweetest sound,
Been a long time since that voice had been around.

"I know it's late, but I need to talk to you.
With that other life, thank God, I'm through.
Please forgive me for hurting you so.
Do you want me? It's all right if you say no."

"Something really strange happened to me tonight,
Under her tree decorated with lights so bright.
'Divorce your wife,' my friends all told me to do.
But tonight, I looked at that manger, God said NO!"

Then Santa came not in a sleigh, but in an old car.
I watched him unpack; "God, he's been so far."
My gifts arrived not carefully wrapped and tagged,
But were those things he brought home in a bag.

It was morning when up from our knees we came.
My Christmas prayer is for you to have the same.
If this Christmas Eve, you're sad and alone,
Remember God's promise:

PRODIGALS DO COME HOME!

We take captive every thought to make it obedient to Christ." 2 Corinthians 10:5

Christmas is over! When Bob and I came home from our daughter's house Christmas evening, we were exhausted. We put away the food, cleaned up the kitchen, sat down, and fell asleep in our chairs.

I can remember and imagine what must have been going on in your mind yesterday and today. What has my spouse been doing? Where? Who was he with all Christmas day?

Some of you know where your spouses have been. Others do not have any idea, so the enemy comes in to give you many negative thoughts and ideas.

May today and this weekend YOU choose to BELIEVE what your Lord has shown, directed, and encouraged you to do regarding your marriage.

As Mary said in *Luke 1:45: "Blessed is she who has believed that what the Lord has said to her will be accomplished!"*

He is always wrestling in prayer for you, that you may stand firm in all the will of God, mature and fully assured. Colossians 4:12

Our prayer for you this weekend, during your quiet time with the Lord, is you will receive a NEW scripture or word from the Lord directing you more completely with assurance that the Lord is working on your marriage.

Jesus answered, "I did tell you, but you do not believe. The miracles I do in my Father's name speak for me." John 10:25

Do not let the enemy steal the joy and meaning of your Christmas! Remember, your Lord is on your side.

And my God will meet all your needs according to his glorious riches in christ Jesus. Philippians 4:19

Christmas is over! Today in the newspaper and on television we'll be tempted to buy bargains this weekend after Christmas!

Although we all may be tempted, my suggestion is for us to each check our checkbook and our hearts. Do we really "need" those items we want to buy? Many are struggling to pay bills and meet all their obligations.

We are praying for all standers that our Lord God will become your Jehovah-jireh; "The Lord will provide." One of your goals this new year might be to get out of debt. You may say that sounds impossible since you're alone, but pray about it. See what the Lord would have you do. Do your part and don't overspend.

Read Genesis 22:1-19.

Our Lord provided for Abraham when God told him to take Isaac on a mountain and sacrifice him as a burnt offering. Our Lord will provide for you and your family in ways you and I can't even imagine.

Remember, our Father, Jehovah-jireh, knows your needs. He instructs us to pray, *"Give us this day our daily bread." Matthew 6:11*

The enemy is coming against so many of God's people through financial problems. May you each ask the Lord to show you what you need to do about your own personal obligations. Don't forget that with God nothing is impossible--even finances!

"So do not worry, saying, 'What shall we eat?' or 'What shall we drink?' or 'What shall we wear?'....But seek first his kingdom and his righteousness, and all these things will be given to you as well." Matthew 6:31, 33

I waited patiently for the Lord; he turned to me and heard my cry. He lifted me out of the slimy pit, out of the mud and mire; he set my feet on a rock and gave me a firm place to stand. He put a new song in my mouth, a hymn of praise to our God. Many will see and fear and put their trust in the Lord." Psalm 40:1-3

Doing God's will sometimes means waiting patiently. While we wait, we can love God, serve Him and tell others about Him.

Waiting for God is not easy. David received four benefits waiting on the Lord. God lifted him out of his despair, set his feet on a rock, gave him a firm place to stand, and put a new song of praise in his mouth.

Often, we can not receive a blessing unless we go through the trial of waiting. Do you have a new song in your heart? Many are watching, and your testimony will help others trust in the Lord.

We are planning to have a couple, from Kentucky with a restored marriage, share their testimony at the New Year's Eve Teleconference. While speaking to the wife tonight, she commented that it was well worth waiting to have her husband back home! We need to totally trust our Lord to know His timing will be perfect!

Wait for the Lord; be strong and take heart and wait for the Lord. Psalm 27:14

♥ NEW YEARS ♥

HAPPY NEW YEAR!

This is another "Bob Cares Also" evening. My wife and several of her standers are busy cleaning up after our New Year's celebration.

Many, starting with Bob, were touched tonight as standers from around the nation celebrated New Year's together by teleconference. Don and Lynn, from Kentucky, gave their testimony of how God is restoring their marriage.

One of Don's comments struck something within me. He spoke of sensing when Lynn was praying for him, while he was a prodigal husband. I know exactly what he means. It scares us, yet it gives us great comfort to know the spouse we have wronged is pleading on our behalf before God.

Does your absent mate know when you are praying? Do things happen, or not happen, when you pray? This morning, New Year's Day, many standers will be tempted to forget to pray. "After all, it's a holiday, and besides, what difference does it make?" Take the word of two returned prodigals, living a thousand miles apart, Don and I know that a praying spouse makes all the difference.

Our ministry theme for 1998 is, "Serious About Standing." Today could be the day of your breakthrough, so don't forget to pray.

Then Jesus told his disciples a parable to show them that they should always pray and not give up." Luke 18:1

Be "Serious About Standing."

Are you serious about standing for your marriage? Have you made a commitment, which is a pledge or a promise, to your marriage regardless of your circumstances? When you said your marriage vows, did you mean the words, "For better or worse, for richer or poorer, in sickness and in health, 'til death us do part?"

When you are PREPARED TO WAIT FOREVER-- THE WAITING DOESN'T TAKE OR SEEM LONG AT ALL.

God is FAITHFUL. As a songwriter wrote, "It is no secret what God can do." He will do it again. He wants to renew, or restore, which means to make new. Believe that your Lord can change your spouse's heart.

"I will give them an undivided heart and put a new spirit in them; I will remove from them their heart of stone and give them a heart of flesh. Then they will follow my decrees and be careful to keep my laws. They will be my people, and I will be their God." Ezekiel 11:19-20

"Then the nations around you that remain will know that I the Lord have rebuilt what was destroyed and have replanted what was desolate. I the Lord have spoken, and I will do it." Ezekiel 36:36

Did you make a New Year's resolution? I usually don't. Like most people, it's often for something I stop doing within a few days.

May I suggest that we all make a New Year's resolution together? I am almost afraid to say this in case I fail, but I think you will be good for my accountability.

What is the New Year's resolution? Have you guessed? Have you read a book this year? I have. In fact, I've read several. It is pretty funny when your husband and friends go to the Christian Bookstore and the clerks know what I like and dislike! But, did I read the Bible through last year? NO! I really feel like the Lord wants me to make this commitment. What about you?

Oh, you and I could justify and say we have read and studied many books of the Bible. Yet, I never have read the Bible all the way through. There, I did it. I confessed it to you! I have wanted to, I have started many times, but still I have never read the Bible completely. So, regardless of how busy my schedule may be, I am going to resolve to read the entire Bible this year. I challenge you to read with me.

I want to read the entire Bible so that I can better understand the scriptures, the history, and the events of the Bible. I know if I do this, the Lord will still speak to me regardless of what book of the Bible I am currently reading. Want to join me?

My heart's desire is for all your marriages to be restored. While we stand, pray, and wait, let's develop a closer, more dependent, and intimate relationship with our Lord and Savior, Jesus Christ.

There are many ways you can read the Bible in a year. There are Bibles arranged in 365 daily readings and there are reading charts to guide you.

I would love to know if you are joining me. By the

way, I have not started, but will use this weekend to get on a schedule. How about you?

All scripture is God-breathed and is useful for teaching, rebuking, correcting and training in righteousness, so that the man of God may be throughly equipped for every good work. 2 Timothy 3:16-17

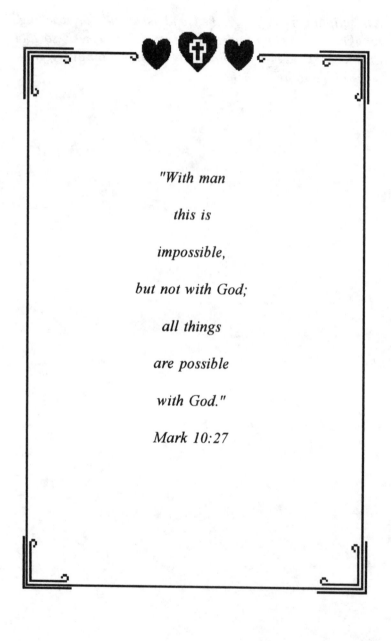

"With man

this is

impossible,

but not with God;

all things

are possible

with God."

Mark 10:27

INTRODUCING

REJOICE MINISTRIES, INC.

"SHARING GOOD NEWS FOR EVERY MARRIAGE"

What Is The Problem?

ONE MAN AND ONE WOMAN FOR A LIFETIME is God's perfect plan for marriage given to us in the Bible. The divorce rate in the United States is above 50 percent. Men and women who once stood at an altar before God and pledged to each other "for better, for worse, for richer, for poorer, in sickness and in health, to love and to cherish, *til death do us part"* are leaving home to pursue selfish desires. They become prodigals, leaving behind brokenhearted children and wounded spouses. Many go on to other marriages, the large percentage of which also fail. Divorce is also attacking families within the church. Satan is out to steal, kill, and destroy families and marriages.

What Is The Provision?

There is a solution to the divorce problem. Our Lord Jesus Christ can heal hurting marriages, even when only one of those involved turns to Christ, seeking marriage restoration. *REJOICE MINISTRIES, INC.* was born out of the needs of hurting couples. All across our nation are thousands of spouses who are standing and praying for God to restore their marriages. We invite you to allow us to stand and pray with you for the restoration of your marriage and home, regardless of circumstances.

THE STEINKAMPS

We were divorced after 19 years of marriage. Our three children became victims of a broken home as Bob became a prodigal spouse and left for the far country. Neither of us realized that satan desires to break up families and destroy marriages.

Charlyne searched the scriptures and discovered that God hates divorce. She found that our Lord Jesus Christ restores and rebuilds marriages, when a mate will love the prodigal unconditionally, as Christ loves us. Charlyne committed herself to a sacrificial stand for the restoration of our marriage. To the glory of God, we were remarried to each other on July 7, 1987.

Today, God allows our family to minister His love, forgiveness, and restoration to others with broken marriages. A newsletter is distributed nationwide. An army of prayer partners pray daily by name for those with hurting marriages. We also maintain a 24-Hour Encouragement Line for spouses standing for God's restoration of their marriages. We desire to be an encouragement as you stand for the healing of your marriage.

"But blessed is the man who trusts in the Lord, whose confidence is in him." Jeremiah 17:7

DO YOU REALLY WANT

A

DIVORCE?

<u>There Is Help Available</u>

* Books and tapes to encourage you in your stand for marriage healing and restoration

* Bible study material to help you learn and grow in God's word

* Newsletters

* Prayer partners to stand and agree with you in prayer

* Testimonies of others with restored marriages to encourage you

"Be strong and courageous. Do not be afraid or terrified...for the Lord your God goes with you; he will never leave you nor forsake you." Deuteronomy 31:6

REJOICE MARRIAGE MINISTRIES
Bob and Charlyne Steinkamp
P.O. Box 11242
Pompano Beach, Florida 33061

(954) 941-6508
FAX (954) 781-7076
Encouragement Line (954) 781-5047
Or Visit Our Web Site At:
www.rejoiceministries.org

May The Lord Bless You And Your Family

ADDITIONAL MATERIAL
AVAILABLE FROM
REJOICE MARRIAGE MINISTRIES

OTHER BOOKS BY
ROBERT AND CHARLYNE STEINKAMP

* "Prodigals Do Come Home"
* "The Twelve Days Of....?"
* "Thoughts On Restoring A Marriage"
* "After The Prodigal Returns
      Standing After The Prodigal Returns"
* "More Thoughts On Restoring A Marriage"
* "Chicagoman"
* "Good News Online"

TAPES BY ROBERT AND CHARLYNE STEINKAMP

* The Steinkamp's Testimony
* Potential Prodigal
* "Unshackled" Radio Testimony
* Prayer (Set of three tapes)
* He Set The Captives Free
* Are You Willing To Pay The Price?
* Study In Ephesians (Set of seven tapes)
* Standing For God's Best
* The Sovereignty Of God
* Don't Give Up!   * He Is The Deliverer
* Repentance   * Hope
* Forgiveness   * Who Are You Like?
* Testimonies   * Are You Different?
* What Is Love?   * Don't Lose Hope
* Anger   * Faith
* Walk In Victory   * Trust
* Prodigal To Prodigal By Robert Steinkamp

YOUR RESPONSE

REJOICE MARRIAGE MINISTRIES
Bob and Charlyne Steinkamp
P. O. Box 11242
Pompano Beach, Florida 33061

___Please add me to the newsletter mailing list.

___Please send information on marriage restoration.

___I want to help.

Enclosed is my donation $_____(tax deductible)

(Please Print Plainly)

NAME
_____

ADDRESS
_____

CITY, STATE, ZIP CODE
_____

PHONE   E-MAIL
_____

MY SPOUSE'S NAME
_____

MY PRAYER REQUEST
_____

_____

Be joyful always; pray continually; give thanks in all circumstances, for this is God's will for you in Christ Jesus. I Thessalonians 5:16-18

THE GREATEST NEWS

That if you confess with your mouth, "Jesus is Lord," and believe in your heart that God raised him from the dead, you will be saved. Romans 10:9

Many have found the first step in a healed marriage to be a personal relationship with Jesus Christ. Our God and creator is waiting to hear your prayer. Have you received Jesus Christ as Lord and Savior of your life? He will save you and be your Comforter and Counselor in the days ahead, regardless of the circumstances.

A Prayer For You

Dear Jesus, I believe that you died for me and that you rose again on the third day. I confess to you that I am a sinner and that I need your love and forgiveness. Come into my life, forgive me for my sins, and give me eternal life. I confess to you now as my Lord and Savior. Thank you for my salvation. Lord, show me your will and your way for my marriage. Mold me and make me to be the spouse I need to be for my spouse. Thank you for rebuilding my marriage. Amen.

Signed_____

Date_____

"Believe in the Lord Jesus, and you will be saved--you and your household. Acts 16:31

MY THOUGHTS

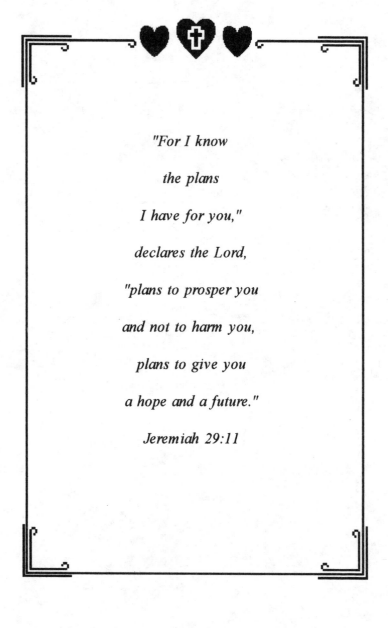

"For I know

the plans

I have for you,"

declares the Lord,

"plans to prosper you

and not to harm you,

plans to give you

a hope and a future."

Jeremiah 29:11